Y0-CUO-312

Date: 2/14/23

**PALM BEACH COUNTY
LIBRARY SYSTEM**

**3650 Summit Boulevard
West Palm Beach, FL 33406**

PECANS
from **SOUP** *to* **NUTS**

DISCARDED:

OUTDATED, REDUNDANT
MATERIAL

PECANS
from SOUP *to* NUTS

Keith Courrégé *and* Marcelle Bienvenu

Photography by Sara Essex

PELICAN PUBLISHING COMPANY
Gretna 2019

When my grandfather Keith Courrégé published his book Pecans from Soup to Nuts *in 1984, he dedicated it to his wife, Betty, and his children, Joe, Dan, and Kay. Sadly, Keith, his wife, and son Dan (my father) are no longer with us.*

Because many of Keith's recipes appear in this new publication, I think it is fitting that this book be dedicated in memoriam to Keith, a bon vivant and great cook. This book is also a tribute to his wife, Joe and Kay, and, of course, to my father and our extended family, all of whom enjoy these delicious pecan-based recipes.

—Jady Regard
Keith Courrégé's grandson

This book is also dedicated to the many cooks, especially my parents, who shared their recipes with me and taught me how to appreciate good food.

—Marcelle Bienvenu

Copyright © 2009
By Jady Regard and Marcelle Bienvenu
All rights reserved

First edition, September 2009
First paperback edition, February 2019

The word "Pelican" and the depiction of a pelican are trademarks of Pelican Publishing Company, Inc., and are registered in the U.S. Patent and Trademark Office.

Library of Congress Cataloging-in-Publication Data

Courrégé, Keith.
  Pecans from soup to nuts / Keith Courrégé and Marcelle Bienvenu ; photography by Sara Essex.
      p. cm.
  Includes index.
  ISBN 9781455624829 (paperback : alk. paper) 1. Cookery (Pecans) I. Bienvenu, Marcelle. II. Title.
  TX814.P4C687 2009
  641.6'452—dc22
                              2009014880

Map on pages 126-27 by Mike Reagan

Printed in the United States of America
Published by Pelican Publishing Company, Inc.
1000 Burmaster Street, Gretna, Louisiana 70053
www.pelicanpub.com

Contents

Acknowledgments   7
Introduction   9

Chapter 1
   The Crown Prince of the Nut Kingdom   11

Chapter 2
   Nibbles and Bits   21

Chapter 3
   To Begin   31

Chapter 4
   Mains and Sides   43

Chapter 5
   Sweets for the Sweet   83

   Source Guide   126
   Index   127

Acknowledgments

Our cookbook would simply not be possible if it were not for a handful of experts that collaborated on this project.

First and foremost, I am very thankful for the privilege to have worked with Marcelle Bienvenu. Marcelle has long been known as one of the most accomplished food writers Louisiana has ever served up. Her list of accomplishments and collaborations reads like a who's who here in the South. Most notably is the fact that she coauthored several cookbooks with celebrity chef Emeril Lagasse and has been a contributing food writer for the *Times-Picayune* in New Orleans since 1984. In addition, she has authored several cookbooks and continues to write and blog for numerous other well-known food publications. We are very fortunate that she could lend her expertise to this project knowing that not only was she famous in her own right, but she also was a personal friend of my late grandfather, Keith Courrégé, and was a great fan of his cooking.

The pages in this book would have never come alive had it not been for the elegant and classic photographs by New Orleanian Sara Essex. I forget now how I discovered Sara and her work, but I am thankful for it. Sara was the photographer I always wanted to meet. Her style is evident throughout the book, and as a result, the pecan never looked so good.

As with all projects, many hands were working behind the scenes and most notably were the hands of food stylist Laura Arrowood. Laura made sure all of our recipes were cooked to perfection, detailed, and styled the Southern way. Her attention to detail allowed the food to do all the talking. I am also thankful to Laura's assistants, Betty DiGiovanni, Barbie Cantwell, and Layla Messkoub, without whom, our days and nights would have been much longer.

Many thanks also to the staff at Pelican Publishing for

their patience and guidance throughout this project.

And finally, thanks to my grandfather Keith Courrégé, or "Taddeus" as we use to lovingly refer to him. He wrote the original version of this cookbook. He was a great cook and known throughout the Acadiana region of south Louisiana for the many dishes he mastered. Like in many Cajun households, his dinner table was located right in the kitchen, and I was lucky enough to enjoy many good meals at the knee of Taddeus. And from time to time, especially in the fall, we enjoyed fresh pecans in some of those great meals.

Jady Regard
CNO (Chief Nut Officer)
Cane River Pecan Company

Introduction

I've been around the pecan industry my entire life.

In 1978, at the tender age of nine, I opened my first bank account. I was in business for the first time, a legitimate operation with two other business partners, my brothers, Danny and Andre. Together, we started The Nutcrackers in the garage of our family home in New Iberia, Louisiana. It was a pecan-cracking operation that remained in business until my younger brother left for college.

Lucky for us, Louisiana is known for having what is referred to as a very large "yard crop." These are the pecans that are harvested by the locals from trees in their yards, which can provide a bountiful harvest.

Usually a few pounds are kept for roasting with salt and butter (great for snacks), or to make pecan pies, creamy pralines, and other pecan-based delights to serve during the fall and winter seasons. If there is an exceptional harvest, the surplus is bagged and sold to local produce markets to provide a bit of extra holiday spending money.

Growing up in a pecan-rich environment, my brothers and I thought that by offering the service of cracking pecans to families who kept some for their personal consumption, we would have our own small business by which to put some change in our pockets. Our theory was correct!

I can't remember a time when pecans were not a part of my life. My father, Dan, acquired a two thousand-acre pecan orchard along the banks of the Cane River in Natchitoches Parish in 1969, the year I was born. Since that time, my entire family has had their hand in the business at one time or another.

In the mid-1980s, my father opened Cane River Pecan Company on historic Front Street in downtown Natchitoches to sell his pecans directly from the orchard. Years later, my mother, Margie, began a corporate mail-order gift division of the company, servicing large corporations that choose to give pecans as holiday gifts. My brothers and I worked side-by-side with my father in the orchards removing limbs, picking pecans, sewing sacks, and loading trucks before launching The Nutcrackers. For a brief time, my younger sister joined our corporate sales division where she landed some of our larger and more influential customers.

The last few years, I have been at the helm of our family's pecan company, establishing sales through our mail-order, Internet, and wholesale efforts. Just when we think the company has grown enough or we have a suitable assortment of pecan goods, a new idea begins to take shape.

This book is one of those ideas.

My grandfather, the late Keith Courrégé, was known as a great cook, and in south Louisiana that means a lot. He was as good with the Cajun basics such as gumbos and étouffées as he was with dishes that are more exotic like his award-winning Sweet-and-Sour Pineapple Salad.

In 1984, he penned the first edition of *Pecans from Soup to Nuts* for our Cane River Pecan Company store in Natchitoches, Louisiana. Because of its popularity, the book has been reprinted several times. Now we bring you a completely updated version of that same cookbook, with new recipes contributed by famed south Louisiana cook and author Marcelle Bienvenu and beautiful photography by Louisiana photographer Sara Essex. This book is a rare collaboration of great talent on the sole subject of pecans.

Throughout the United States, the use of pecans is nearly religious. There is hardly a fall or winter celebration that goes by that scores of these sweet nuts are not consumed in the form of pies or pralines, included in casseroles and cakes, or featured simply as a roasted treat. The pecan is America's favorite nut, and it's no wonder that the nut has been touted as God's gift to the South.

I am proud to introduce a collection of simple but delicious recipes, all of which feature pecans. We at Cane River Pecan Company hope that everyone will have the opportunity to enjoy this great nut in the book's featured recipes or, perhaps, naturally right out of the shell.

Jady Regard
CNO (Chief Nut Officer)
Cane River Pecan Company

Chapter 1
The Crown Prince of the Nut Kingdom

Is it PEE-CANS or PA-KAWNS?

It really doesn't matter how you say the name of the nut, pecans have long been enjoyed in copious culinary delights: roasted with butter and salt; candied with sugar and other flavorings; added to soups; tossed in salads; used to crust meats, seafood, and poultry; stirred into cake batters and frostings; and utilized in a plethora of pies, candies, and cookies.

When Keith Courrégé, a pecan connoisseur and culinary aficionado of the highest order, self-published his book *Pecans from Soup to Nuts* in 1984, he proclaimed that the pecan was the "Crown Prince of the Nut Kingdom, God's gift to the South." Indeed, it's the Southern states that are the largest producers and consumers of this delicious, versatile nut, and for this reason, many pecan-based delicacies have become a staple in Southern cuisine.

The history of the pecan began thousands of years before the discovery of America. It is believed that certain North American Indian tribes were the only people who knew about pecan trees. No one from any other part of the world had ever seen this nut. In 1787, Thomas Walton, an Englishman who had a plantation in South Carolina, described the foliage of the pecan but ended with "the fruit I have not seen."

History tells us that George Washington planted pecan trees at Mount Vernon. The trees were a gift from Thomas Jefferson, who is credited with their initial popularity in the South. Washington was fond of the pecans and constantly enjoyed them when they were available from his orchard. In a diary entry dated 1794, he mentioned planting "several poccon, or Illinois nuts."

Some fifty years later at Oak Alley Plantation, owned by Telesphore J. Roman and located along the great River Road in Louisiana, a slave gardener known only by his given name Antoine succeeded in grafting sixteen trees near the plantation mansion in 1846 or 1847. Later, he successfully grafted 110 trees. This was an epoch in the history of pecan growing since it was the first successful effort of record to graft pecan trees. It was also the first commercial orchard developed to produce nuts for sale.

Thanks to Antoine, the pecan industry developed and now, more than 150 years later, pecan orchards continue to flourish in Louisiana. Drive along Louisiana Highway 1, from Alexandria (where some claim there is an imaginary line that separates north and south Louisiana) to Natchitoches, and you'll see grand majestic pecan orchards lining both sides of the road as far as the eye can see. It was near Natchitoches, on the Cane River, where pecan orchards thrived alongside vast cotton fields, that Dan Regard first got into the pecan business in 1969. Years later, he opened Cane River Pecan Company, on Front Street in downtown Natchitoches, as an outlet to sell his pecans directly from the orchard. The town, which predates the 1718 founding of New Orleans, and the

languorous river are surrounded by historic plantations, Creole architecture, and huge, stately oak trees.

Spring, in Louisiana, is said to have arrived only when the first bright green leaves appear on the stark bare limbs of the pecan trees. In a matter of days, or so it seems, the leaves fill out and the trees bask in their glory. During the spring and summer, the pecan trees provide shade under which there are picnics, barbecues, and all manner of warm-weather gatherings. It is also the time that commercial growers tend to the orchard, checking the trees for disease, trimming dead or damaged limbs, and sprucing up the grounds.

In the fall, when the cold fronts begin pushing their way south, gusty autumn winds send the dry, crackly leaves and the mature nuts flying, and the nut-loaded limbs are soon bare. The locals then scramble, sometimes on their hands and knees, to pick pecans to load into sacks and baskets in hopes of selling them. However, they always keep some for their personal larder to make goodies for the winter holidays.

At commercial farms, pecan growers are busy clearing the orchards. Fallen limbs are removed to allow heavy commercial harvesting equipment to sweep the orchard floor. Until the early 1980s, pecans in the Regard orchards were hand picked, but now mechanized equipment is used.

Harvesting usually begins the second or third week in October and can last, depending on the size of a farm or orchard, up to eight to ten weeks. During harvesting, small sticks, nuts, and even small rocks will be gathered at one time. Of course, inclement weather always seems to creep up on a good harvest. Thunderstorms roar through, sometimes causing wind damage to the trees. Tractors get stuck in the mud. Equipment breaks down.

Once the harvest is completed, the gathered nuts are sorted according to size and packaged for their journey to a commercial sheller. It may take a commercial sheller up to six months to shell his purchased nuts. End users, including grocery chains, candy makers, ice cream producers, bakeries, and food service companies, buy the shelled pecans.

All unsold pecans are kept in cold storage, where they do very well until the following year. Unbeknownst to most consumers, pecans purchased at major supermarkets in the fall and winter months are actually from the previous year's crop, which has been held in cold storage.

It takes ten years for a pecan tree to produce a profitable crop. One tree alone can yield up to four hundred pounds of nuts in a good year. In the United States, pecans are second in popularity only to peanuts (which are not even true nuts). The United States produces about eighty percent of the world's pecans.

The Good Nutritional News about the Pecan

If you're nuts about nuts, there's good news. Pecans are not only tasty, but are also nutritious. They have been found to be an excellent source of protein and contain carbohydrates, which are energy-producing nutrients. Pecans are also a great source of antioxidants and have been shown to prevent LDL (low-density lipoprotein,

also known as the "bad" cholesterol) from building up in arteries, and can help lower total cholesterol levels. Compared to other nuts, pecans have one of the highest levels of phytosterols, a group of plant chemicals that may help protect against cardiovascular disease.

The fat found in pecans is mostly polyunsaturated and contains no cholesterol. Pecans add fiber to your diet and contain nineteen vitamins and minerals, including iron; calcium; vitamins A, B, and C; potassium; and phosphorous. These nuts are flavorful and can add a delightful crunchy texture to a variety of foods. Adding ten large pecan halves to your salads, vegetables, meat dishes, and desserts will add sixty-five nutritious calories to your diet.

Food for thought: One ounce (about nineteen halves) contains 196 calories, 3 grams of protein, and 20 grams of fat. Ninety percent of the fats are unsaturated (about sixty percent monounsaturated and thirty percent polyunsaturated). These nuts are sodium free and fiber rich.

Of course, remember moderation is the key word when consuming all good things.

Storing Pecans

Since pecans are a seasonal crop, you will want to store plenty for year-round use. It's best to harvest pecans as soon as possible after they fall to the ground, as the nuts can deteriorate rapidly if they become wet from rain and high humidity.

To speed up the drying process, arrange the pecans in a single layer in a shallow baking pan or tray and let sit in a warm, dry area for one to two weeks. They should be stored once they are thoroughly dry in airtight containers in a cool, dry, dark place.

Because pecans are rich in oil and will become stale or rancid quickly, they should be stored properly. Shelled or unshelled nuts will keep fresh for about a year stored in airtight containers in the refrigerator or several years in the freezer. Package shelled pecans in moisture/vapor-proof containers, such as plastic cartons, glass freezer

jars, reusable cans, or plastic freezer bags. Pack tightly and exclude as much air as possible. Unbroken kernels stay fresh longer than broken pieces. Nuts can be thawed and refrozen without loss of quality.

Tell Me More!

The recipes in this book may call for different forms of the pecan, so we invite you to acquaint yourself with these terms.

Pecan meal is finely ground pecans. It is primarily used to coat or crust fish, chicken, meats, or vegetables. It can be added to piecrusts, pancake batter, or the batter for frying chicken or fish.

To produce this meal, put pecan halves or pieces in a food processor or electric blender and pulse several times until very fine. **Do not overprocess.** Due to the high oil content, the meal can turn almost into butter if ground too quickly. One cup of pecan halves or pieces yields about one cup of meal. You can make a large batch of the meal and store it in airtight containers in the freezer for later use.

Pecan halves come in various sizes.

Pecan Sizes (halves per pound)
Mammoth = 200-250 halves
Junior mammoth = 251-300 halves
Jumbo = 301-350 halves
Extra large = 351-450 halves
Large = 451-550 halves
Medium = 551-650 halves

Cane River Pecan Company offers only the mammoth size, and the recipes featured in this book use that size pecan. However, any size will do for most applications—just be sure the nuts are fresh and come from a reliable source. Pecan halves are used for decoration or garnish for pies and cakes and for making pralines and other candies.

Chopped pecans are simply halves that are chopped and used in various applications.

Pecan pieces are usually broken pieces of pecans and can be used interchangeably with chopped pecans.

Chapter 2
Nibbles and Bits

Whet your appetite and tickle your taste buds with these delicious and simple snacks. Roasted or sugared pecans are a great alternative to cheese and crackers or chips and dips to serve prior to any meal, and they go well with a glass of wine, a cold beer, or an apéritif.

These nibbles and bits can be made ahead of time and stored in airtight containers until ready to serve.

NOTE: Some recipes call for toasted pecans. To toast, spread pecan halves in a single layer on a baking sheet and bake at 300 degrees for 8 to 10 minutes, depending on the size of the halves. Chopped pecans can be quickly toasted in a hot nonstick skillet over medium heat for 1 to 3 minutes, depending on the degree of toastiness desired.

Basic Roasted Pecans

Roasted pecans are one of the most popular ways of preparing pecans. Just about everyone has his or her method and recipe. There are those who will tell you to roast the nuts quickly in a hot oven, while others prefer the slow-roasting method. Slow roasting is our preference. We also recommend using the largest size pecan halves you can find for this delicious treat. Be aware that the cooking time will vary according to the size of the pecan. Smaller pecans will roast faster than larger ones.

Although roasted pecans are popular for snacking, they can also be chopped and sprinkled on ice cream, yogurt, and fresh fruit. They add a delightful taste and crunch to salads, cereals, and steamed vegetables. Roasted pecan halves can be stuffed into prunes and dates. Serve these with chèvre (goat cheese), Brie, or Gorgonzola for a delicious treat. Or, better yet, roll any soft cheese in chopped roasted pecans and serve with party crackers.

Makes 2 pints

4 cups pecan halves

4 tablespoons butter, melted

1 tablespoon salt

Preheat the oven to 275 degrees.

Spread the pecans evenly in one layer on a heavy baking sheet. Pour the butter over the pecans, stirring to coat evenly. Roast for about 45 minutes, stirring at 15-minute intervals, until desired degree of toastiness is reached.

When done, remove from the oven and sprinkle the salt while the pecans are still warm. Cool completely before storing in airtight containers.

Variations: This is where you can be creative and experiment with various combinations of spices, oils, and condiments. Use these in place of or in addition to the salt in the Basic Roasted Pecan recipe.

Here are some suggestions to give you inspiration:
- 1 teaspoon each of chili powder, onion salt, and cayenne pepper
- 1 teaspoon each of soy sauce, garlic powder, and ground ginger
- 1 teaspoon each of sesame oil, Chinese five-spice powder, and soy sauce
- 1 teaspoon each of Worcestershire sauce, onion powder, and celery salt

Basic Sugared Pecans

Sugar pecans can be served before or after dinner, but they certainly can be chopped to sprinkle on ice cream sundaes, slices of pound cake, or added to fruit smoothies.

Makes 2 pints

2 cups sugar

¾ cup milk

1 tablespoon butter

Pinch of salt

4 cups large pecan halves

1 teaspoon vanilla

Combine the sugar, milk, butter, and salt in a medium-size heavy saucepan over medium heat. Cook, stirring constantly, until the mixture reaches a soft ball stage, 235 to 239 degrees on a candy thermometer.

Add the pecans and vanilla, mix well, and spread on a platter to cool. Separate the pecans with a fork. Store in an airtight container.

Deviled Eggs with Pecans

Deviled eggs are ideal to bring along for picnics and potluck dinners, or to serve at barbecues, but they can be served as well with cocktails prior to a dinner party. For an elegant presentation, fill a pastry bag with the egg-yolk mixture and use a small decorative tip to pipe it into the egg whites. The pecan meal gives the eggs a wonderful texture.

Makes 12

6 hard-boiled eggs, peeled

⅓ cup pecan meal

Dash each of garlic powder and onion powder

½ teaspoon salt

Hot sauce to taste

1 tablespoon dill pickle relish

1 tablespoon sweet pickle relish

2 teaspoons yellow mustard

2 tablespoons mayonnaise

Dill pickle relish for garnish (optional)

Slice the eggs in half lengthwise and gently remove the yolks. Put the yolks and the remaining ingredients in a bowl and mix well. For a smoother mixture, pulse in a food processor. Fill each egg white with an equal amount of the mixture and chill for at least 1 hour before serving. Garnish with relish if you like.

Variation:
6 hard-boiled eggs, peeled
2 tablespoons mayonnaise
1 tablespoon tomato paste
1 tablespoon grated Parmesan cheese
½ teaspoon lemon juice
¼ cup pecan meal
½ teaspoon salt
Hot sauce to taste
Grated Parmesan cheese for garnish (optional)

Slice the eggs in half lengthwise and gently remove the yolks. Put the yolks and the remaining ingredients in a bowl and mix well. For a smoother mixture, pulse in a food processor. Fill each egg white with an equal amount of the mixture and chill for at least 1 hour before serving. Garnish with Parmesan cheese if you wish.

Cheesy Pecan Wafers

Similar to cheese straws, these wafers are from Keith Courrégé's repertoire of recipes. They are ideal to serve during the cocktail hour and make a great food gift during the Christmas holidays.

Makes about 4 dozen

½ pound finely grated sharp cheddar cheese, at room temperature

1 stick (8 tablespoons) butter, softened

1 teaspoon Worcestershire sauce

¼ teaspoon cayenne pepper (or more to taste)

¼ teaspoon salt

1½ cups all-purpose flour

⅛ teaspoon hot sauce (or more to taste)

1¼ cup pecan halves

Preheat the oven to 300 degrees.

Combine the cheese, butter, Worcestershire, cayenne, salt, and flour in a food processor or electric blender and pulse several times to blend. The mixture should be soft and smooth.

Form the mixture into small balls, about the size of a large pecan, and place on an ungreased nonstick cookie sheet. Flatten the balls with the tines of a fork and place a pecan half on each wafer.

Bake until just lightly browned, 25 to 30 minutes. Remove from the oven and cool slightly before transferring to a wire rack to cool completely.

Once the wafers are completely cooled, store them between sheets of wax paper in airtight containers.

Chapter 3
To Begin

Soups and salads don't have to be ho-hum. Add pecans and the dishes can be elevated to new heights. You'll be pleasantly surprised by the flavor and crunch in our onion soup and cream of potato soup.

During the summer months, try adding chopped pecans to chilled fruit soups—wonderful! Experiment with using chopped pecans in all types of salads. They pair especially well with apples, pears, and berries. Roasted chopped pecans bring a great texture and taste as well to coleslaws and fruit compotes.

Onion Soup with Pecan Crust

When the cold, winter winds are blowing, make a pot of this hearty soup to serve on trays in front of a crackling fire. The onions take a while to caramelize, but it's time well spent because the flavor and color make the soup outstanding.

Makes 6 servings

¾ stick (6 tablespoons) butter

5 medium-size yellow onions, thinly sliced

2 tablespoons all-purpose flour

3 cups warm chicken broth

3 cups warm beef consommé

2 tablespoons brandy

6 large slices toasted French bread rubbed with a cut garlic clove

¾ pound Gruyère cheese, grated

¼ cup freshly grated Parmesan cheese

⅓ cup pecan meal

3 tablespoons olive oil

Melt the butter in a large saucepan or soup pot over medium-low heat. Add the onions and cook, stirring often, until golden and caramelized, 30 to 40 minutes.

Add the flour and cook, stirring to blend well, about 2 minutes. Slowly add the warm broth, consommé, and brandy, whisking constantly until blended. Simmer, stirring occasionally, until the mixture thickens, 10 to 12 minutes.

Preheat the broiler. Adjust the oven rack to about 4 inches below the broiler heat.

Place the toasted bread in 6 ovenproof soup bowls or small crocks.

Sprinkle with equal amounts of the cheeses and pecan meal. Drizzle with equal amounts of the olive oil. Pour equal amounts of the soup into the bowls and place the bowls on a large baking sheet and broil until the cheese is melted, 3 to 5 minutes.

Serve hot.

Cream of Potato and Pecan Soup

Whip up a batch of this creamy soup to serve while watching football games or for an informal Sunday-night supper during the winter months. Don't forget to offer hot crusty French bread with each serving.

If you prefer your soup to be a bit thinner, add a little chicken broth with the milk in the preparation.

Makes 6 to 8 servings

1 stick (8 tablespoons) butter

½ cup chopped yellow onions

2 tablespoons all-purpose flour

4 cups milk

1 cup peeled and cubed red-skinned potatoes

2 cups pecan meal

1 garlic clove, crushed

Salt and hot sauce to taste

Pinch of nutmeg

1 cup heavy cream

2 tablespoons chopped parsley

2 tablespoons chopped green onions (green part only)

French bread for serving

Melt the butter in a large saucepan over medium heat. Add the onions and cook, stirring, until soft and golden, about 6 minutes. Add the flour and whisk until the mixture is smooth.

Add the milk, stirring constantly, until the mixture comes to a gentle boil. Reduce the heat to medium low and add the potatoes, pecan meal, and garlic, and season with salt and hot sauce.

Simmer, stirring occasionally, until the potatoes are tender, about 20 minutes. Add the nutmeg and gradually add the cream, stirring constantly until the mixture thickens slightly, about 5 minutes. Add the parsley and green onions.

Ladle into soup bowls and serve immediately with hot French bread.

Egg Salad with Bacon and Pecans

This is great to serve on cool, crisp salad greens, plopped on thick slices of tomatoes, or tucked between the toasted bread of your choice.

Makes 8 servings

12 hard-boiled eggs, peeled and chopped

1 cup finely chopped celery

¼ cup finely chopped green onions (green part only)

¾ pound bacon, chopped, cooked crisp, and drained

2 teaspoons prepared horseradish

1 cup mayonnaise

1 tablespoon Creole mustard

Salt, black pepper, and cayenne pepper to taste

3 tablespoons chopped pecans

½ cup chopped parsley

Combine the eggs, celery, onions, and bacon in a large mixing bowl.

Combine the horseradish, mayonnaise, and Creole mustard and fold into the salad. Season to taste with salt, pepper, and cayenne. Add the pecans and parsley and mix gently.

Serve at room temperature or chilled.

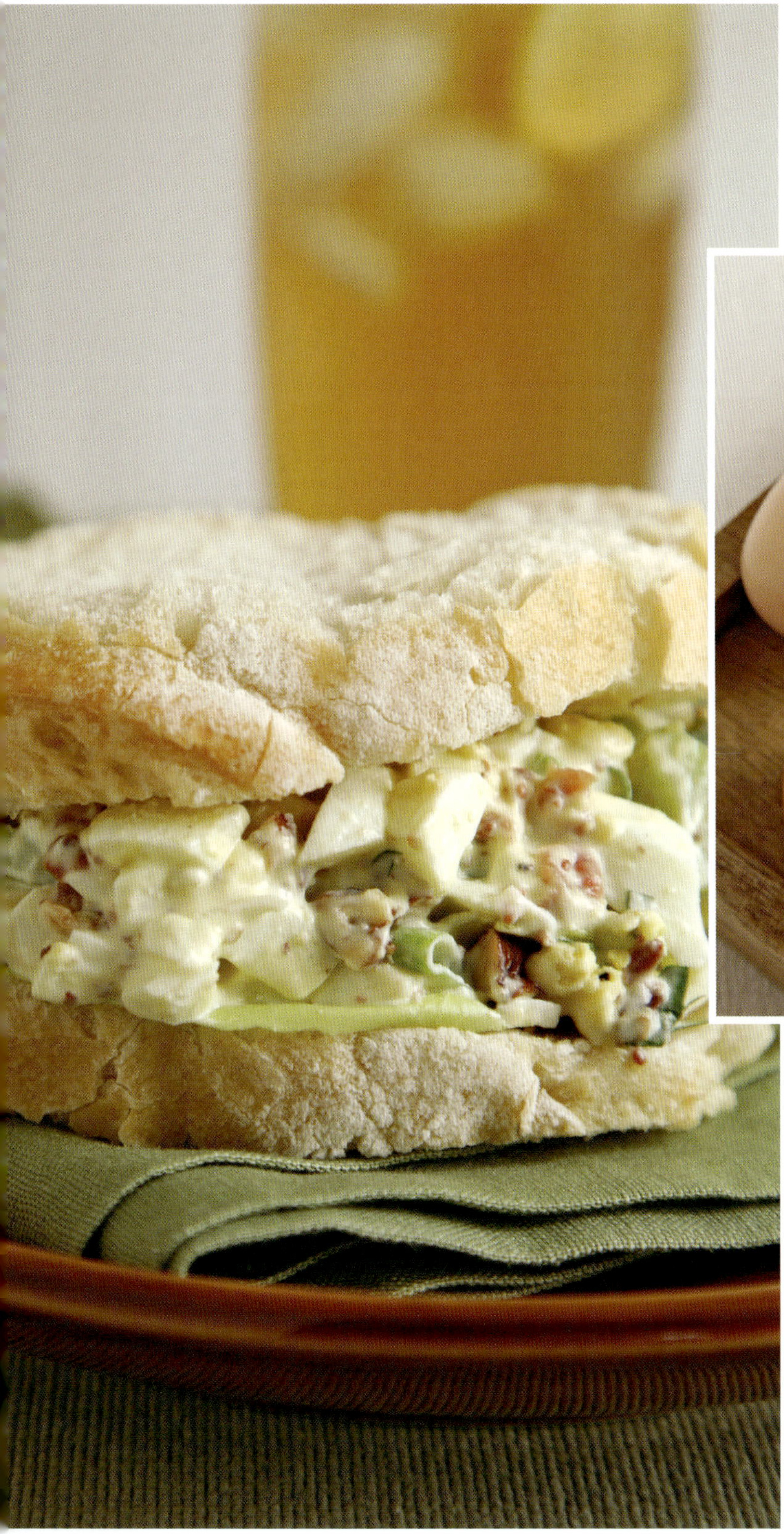
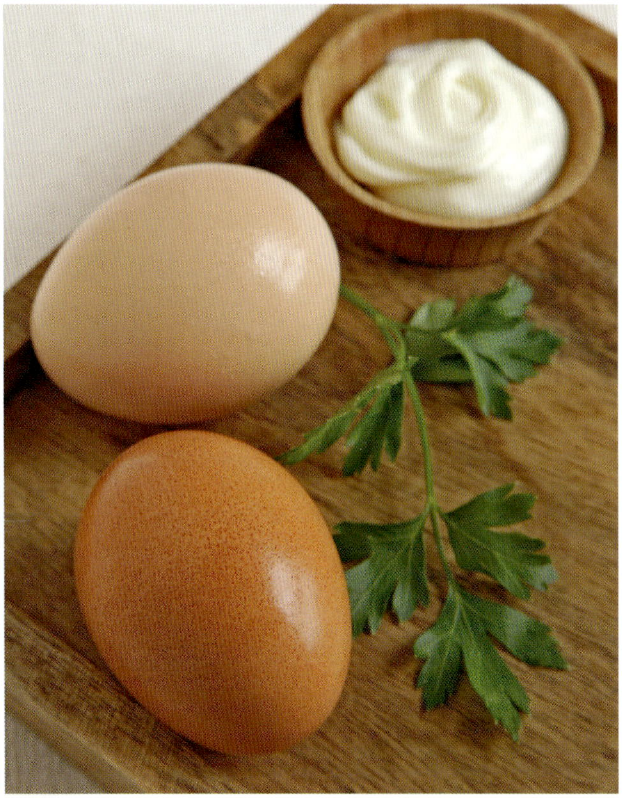

Pecan and Chicken Salad

Chicken salad has long been a Southern favorite to serve at parties and family gatherings. It's versatile and can be spread on bread to make sandwiches, served in halved avocados, or stuffed into vine-ripened tomatoes. The addition of the pecans turns a good chicken salad into a great one.

Makes 4 servings

2 hard-boiled eggs, finely chopped

2 cups finely chopped cooked chicken breasts

3 teaspoons finely chopped fresh parsley leaves

⅓ cup mayonnaise (or more to taste)

⅓ cup sour cream

2 teaspoons fresh lemon juice

¼ cup finely chopped celery

¼ cup finely chopped pecans

Salt, freshly ground black pepper, and cayenne pepper to taste

Combine all of the ingredients in a mixing bowl. Cover and chill for at least two hours before serving.

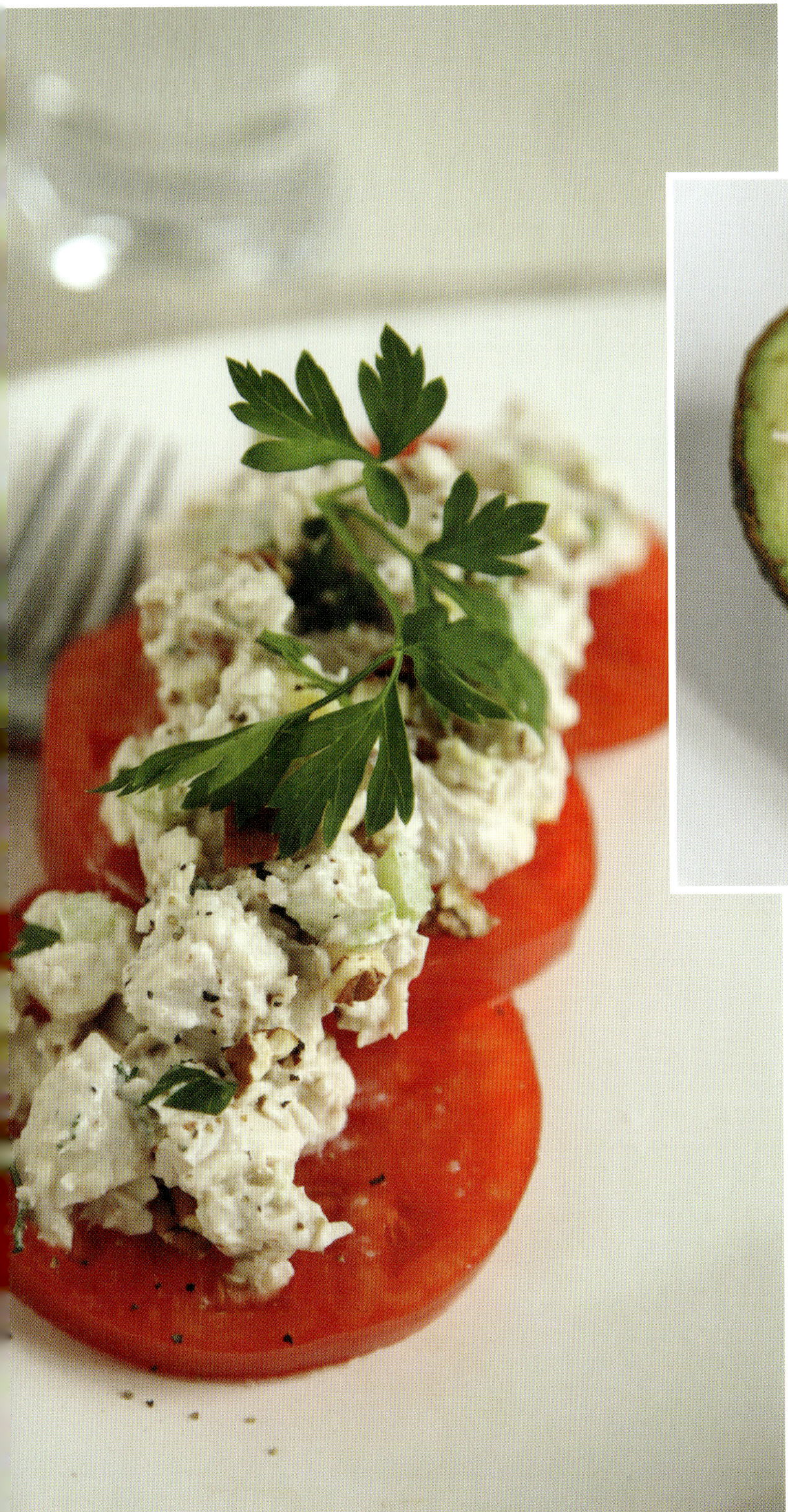

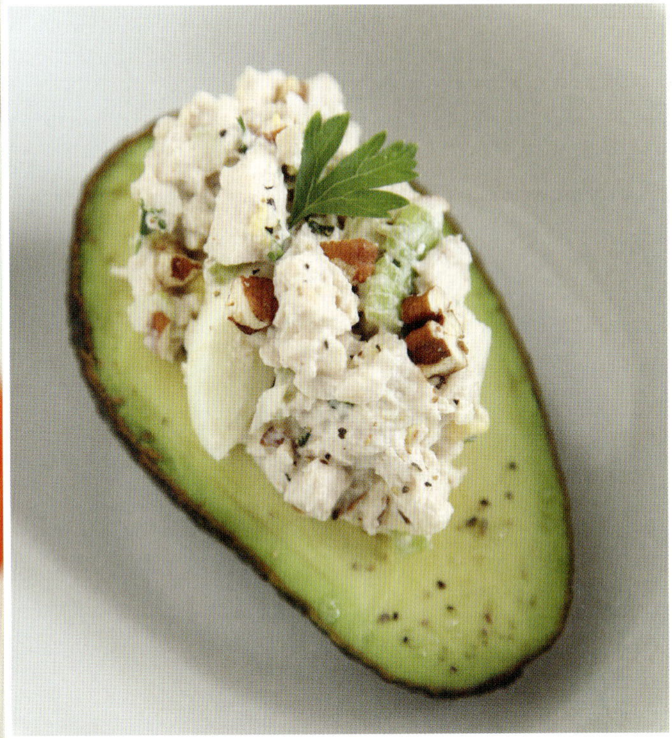

Pear, Roasted Pecans, and Arugula Salad

When pears are in season, this is a delightful salad to serve before a meal of roasted pork or beef. The peppery flavor of the arugula complements the sweetness of the pears, but you can use any salad greens that strike your fancy. The salad is a wonderful palate-cleansing first course.

Makes 6 servings

2 ripe pears, peeled, cored, and coarsely chopped

2 teaspoons plus 2 tablespoons fresh lemon juice

½ cup olive oil

1 teaspoon Dijon mustard

1 tablespoon chopped shallots

Salt and freshly ground black pepper

5 cups baby arugula or other salad greens

½ cup crumbled blue cheese

½ cup roasted and chopped pecans

Toss the pears with 2 teaspoons of the lemon juice and set aside.

In a small clean jar, combine the 2 tablespoons lemon juice, oil, mustard, and shallots. Fit the jar with a lid and shake to blend. Season with salt and pepper. Shake again and set aside.

When ready to serve, put the salad greens in a large bowl, add the pears, cheese, and pecans. Pour in the dressing and toss to coat evenly. Serve immediately.

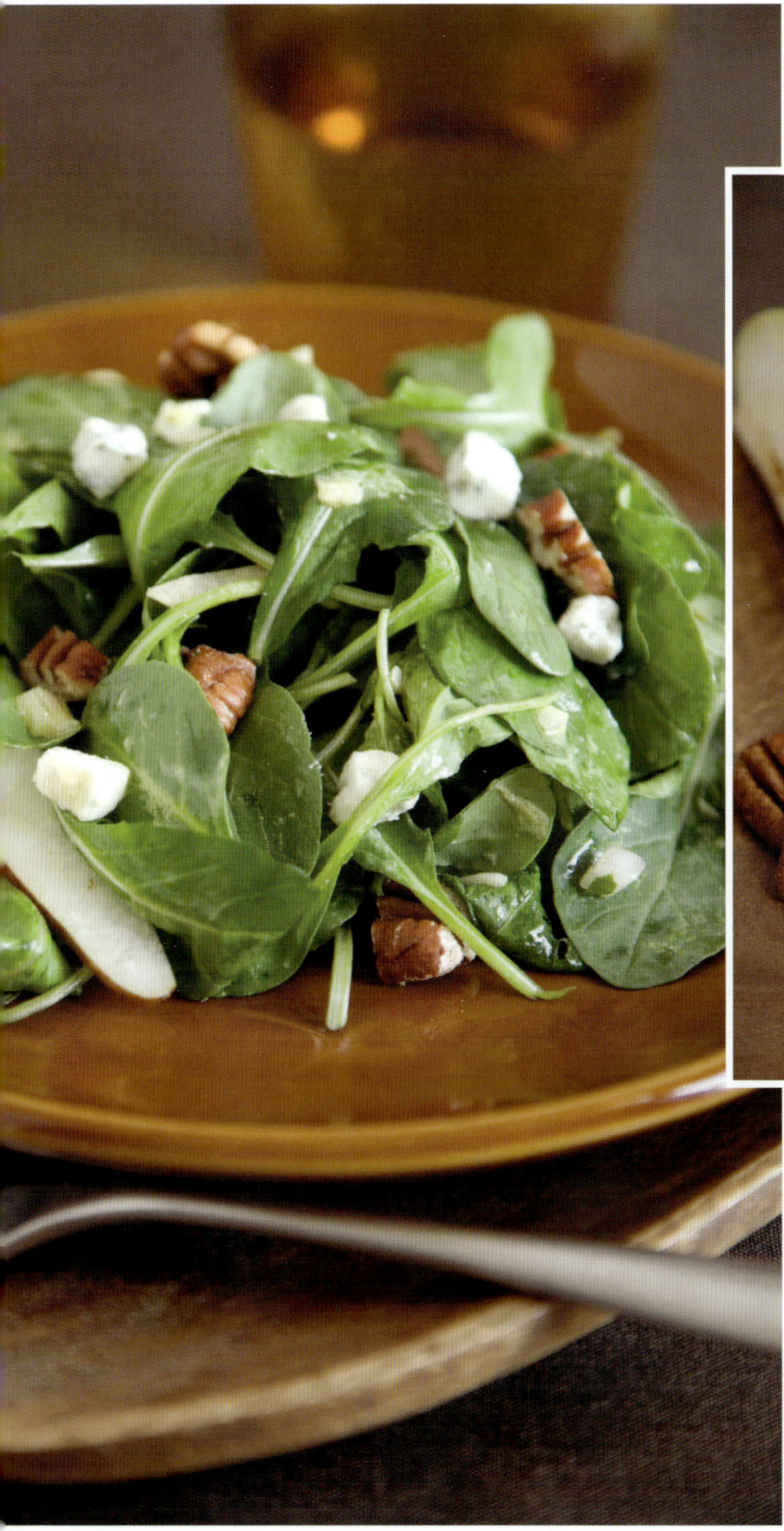
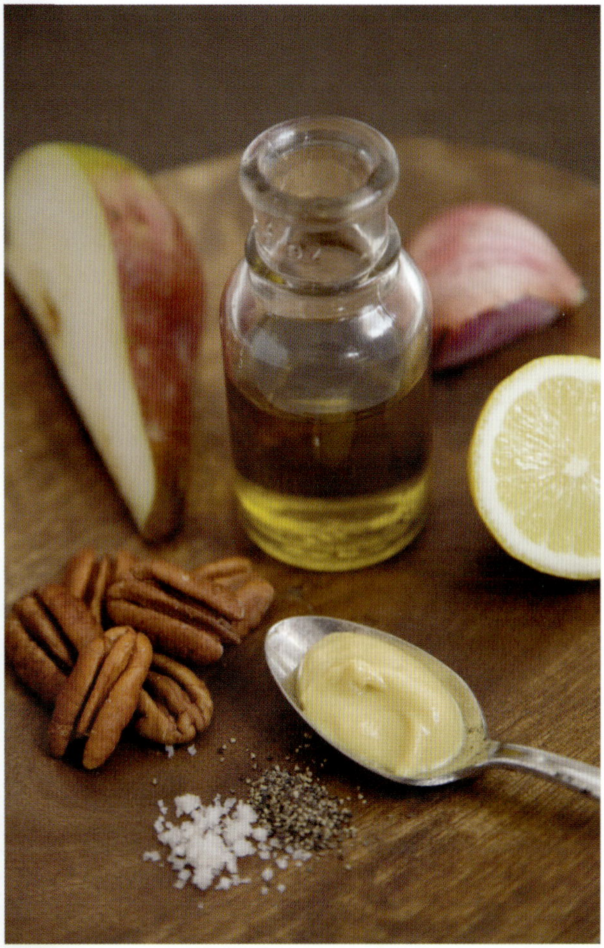

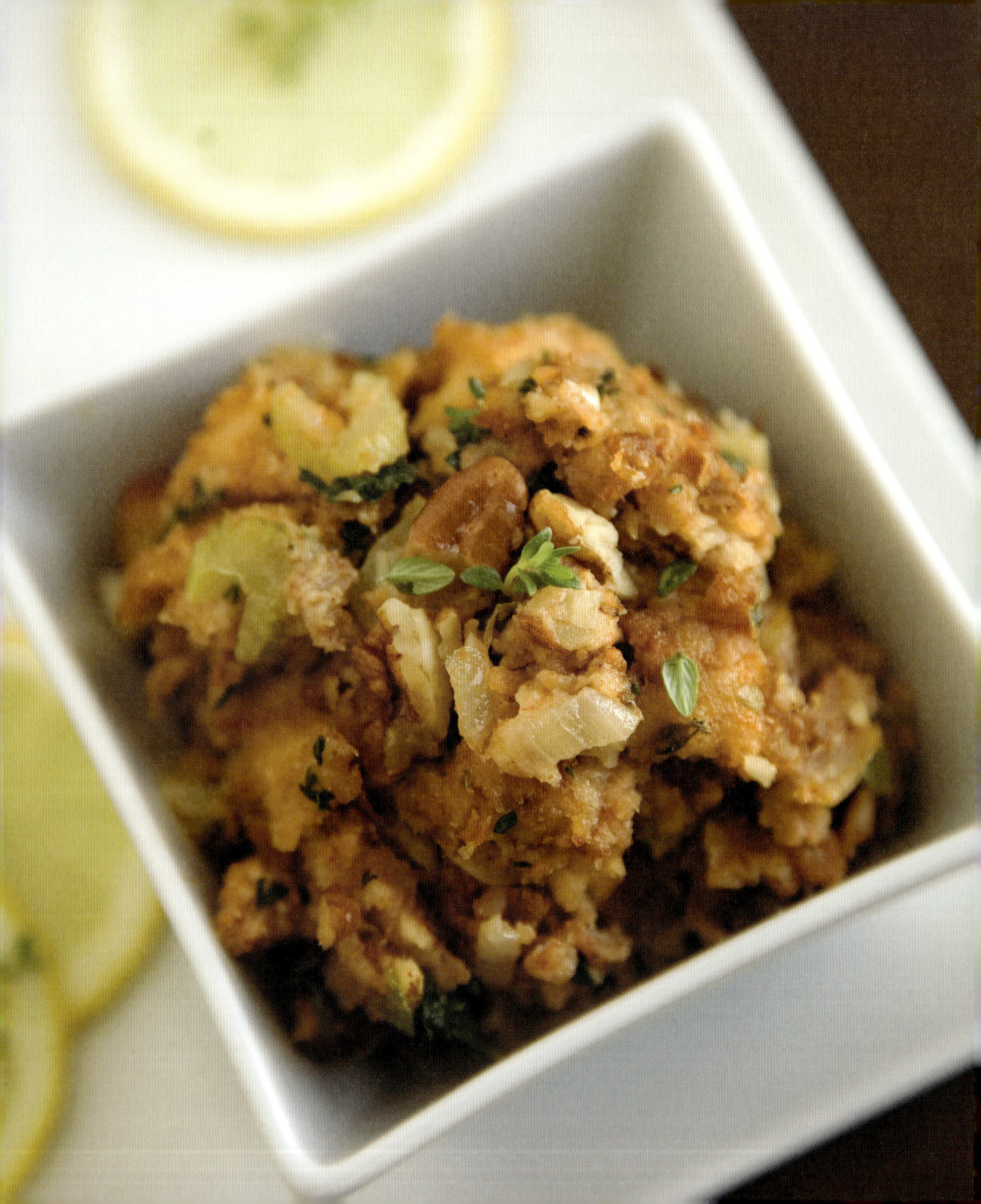

Chapter 4
Mains and Sides

The versatile pecan pairs well with beef, pork, chicken, most seafood, and a wealth of vegetables, especially eggplant, beans, and sweet potatoes. Toss chopped pecans or pecan meal with rice or pasta to add incredible flavor and texture.

In this chapter, main courses are presented with complementary sides, but don't be afraid to change them around and mix and match to find the flavors that please your taste buds.

Baked Pecan Chicken with Lemon Rice Dressing

Dipped first in buttermilk and then dredged in pecan meal, this chicken dish will please just about everyone! We suggest serving it with rice perked up with lemon zest and dill or parsley—a simple but delicious side dish.

Makes 8 servings

1½ sticks butter, melted

1 cup buttermilk

1 egg, beaten

1 cup all-purpose flour

1 cup pecan meal

½ cup grated Parmesan cheese

1 tablespoon sweet paprika

1 tablespoon salt

Cayenne pepper to taste

2 broiler-fryer chickens (each 3½ to 4 pounds), quartered

Preheat the oven to 350 degrees. Pour the butter into a large baking dish and set aside.

Combine the buttermilk and egg in a shallow bowl and whisk to blend.

Combine the flour, pecan meal, Parmesan cheese, paprika, salt, and cayenne in another shallow bowl and stir to blend.

Dip the chicken pieces first in the egg mixture then in the flour mixture, coating evenly. Place the chicken quarters in the prepared baking dish, turning them to coat evenly with the butter. Arrange the chicken pieces in the baking dish, skin side up.

Bake until the chicken is nicely browned and the juices run clear, about 1 hour.

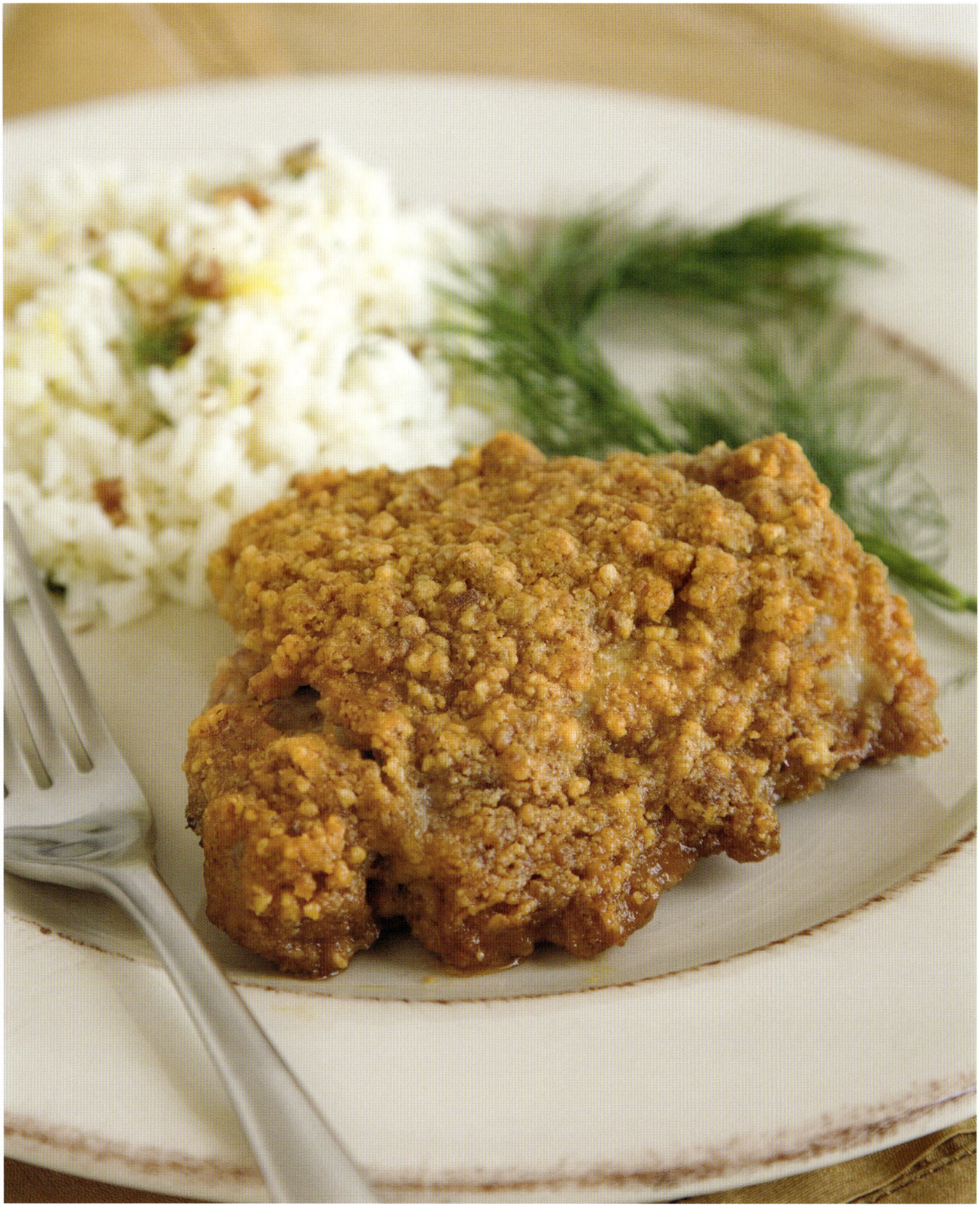

Lemon Rice Dressing

Makes 8 to 10 servings

5 cups chicken broth

1 teaspoon salt

½ teaspoon freshly ground black pepper

¼ teaspoon cayenne pepper

2 garlic cloves, crushed

2 cups long-grain white rice

2 tablespoons freshly grated lemon zest

1 tablespoon chopped fresh dill (or parsley)

3 tablespoons butter

¼ cup toasted chopped pecans

Heat the broth, salt, black pepper, cayenne, and garlic in a large, heavy saucepan and bring the mixture to a boil. Stir in the rice, cover, reduce the heat to medium low and simmer until the liquid is absorbed, 20 to 25 minutes.

Remove from the heat. Stir in the lemon zest and let stand, covered, for 5 minutes. Add the dill (or parsley) and butter. Gently fluff with a fork. Serve warm and garnish with the chopped pecans.

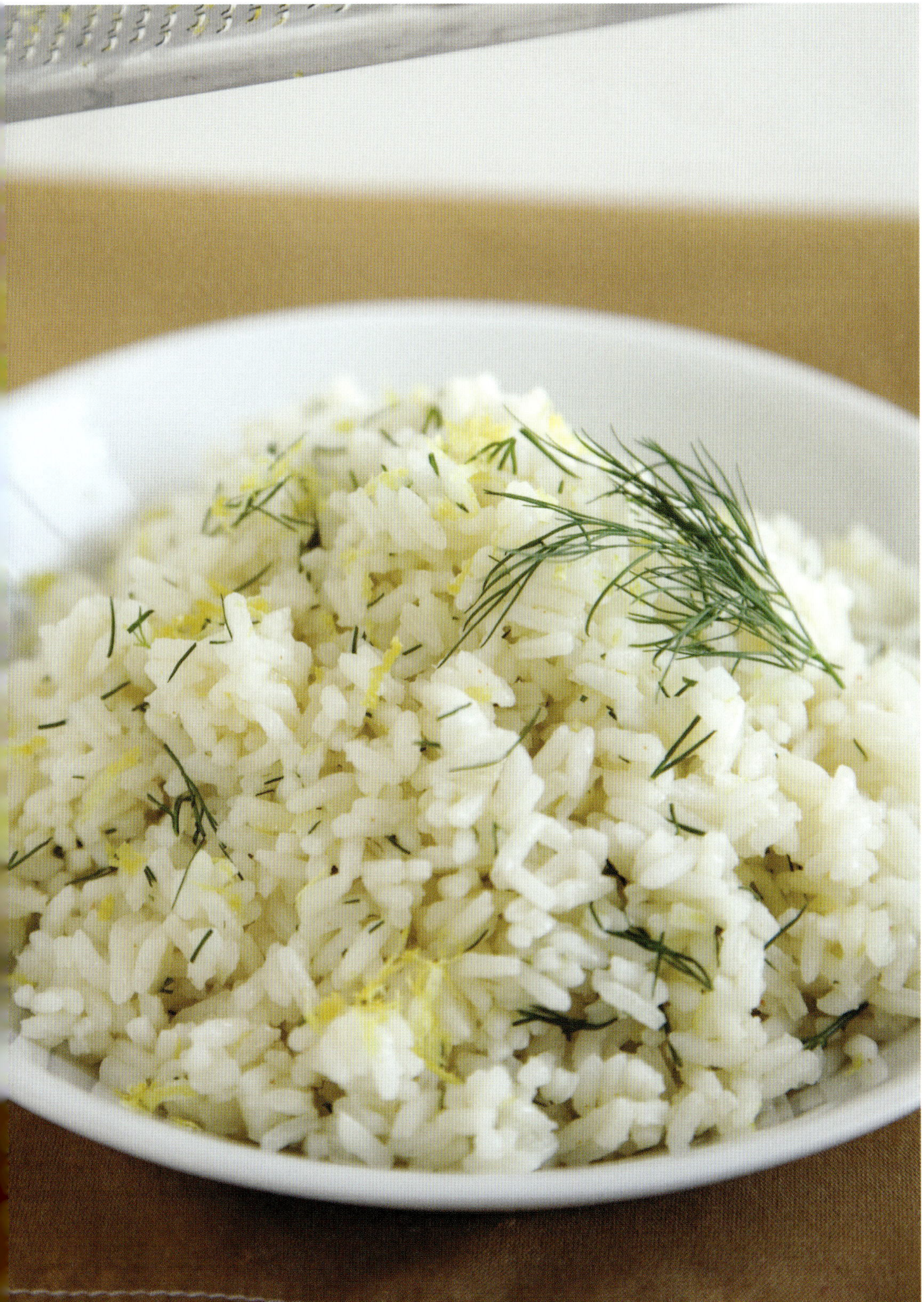

Pecan-Ginger Chicken with Pecan Rice Pilaf

The ginger, honey, soy sauce, and hot mustard give the chicken an Asian flavor.

Makes 4 servings

2 tablespoons pecan meal

2 teaspoons grated fresh gingerroot

2 tablespoons honey

3 tablespoons soy sauce

2 teaspoons (or to taste) Chinese hot mustard

2 tablespoons olive oil

4 chicken breasts (each 6 to 8 ounces), deboned and skinless

8 green onion strips for garnish

Combine the pecan meal, ginger, honey, soy sauce, mustard, and olive oil in a small bowl and stir well. Set aside.

Place the chicken breasts between two sheets of heavy-duty plastic wrap and flatten to about ¼-inch thickness using a meat mallet.

Place the chicken breasts in a shallow bowl and pour in the marinade. Cover and refrigerate for 1 hour.

Remove the chicken from the marinade. Grill over medium-hot coals and baste with the soy sauce mixture until the juices run clear, 2 to 3 minutes on each side.

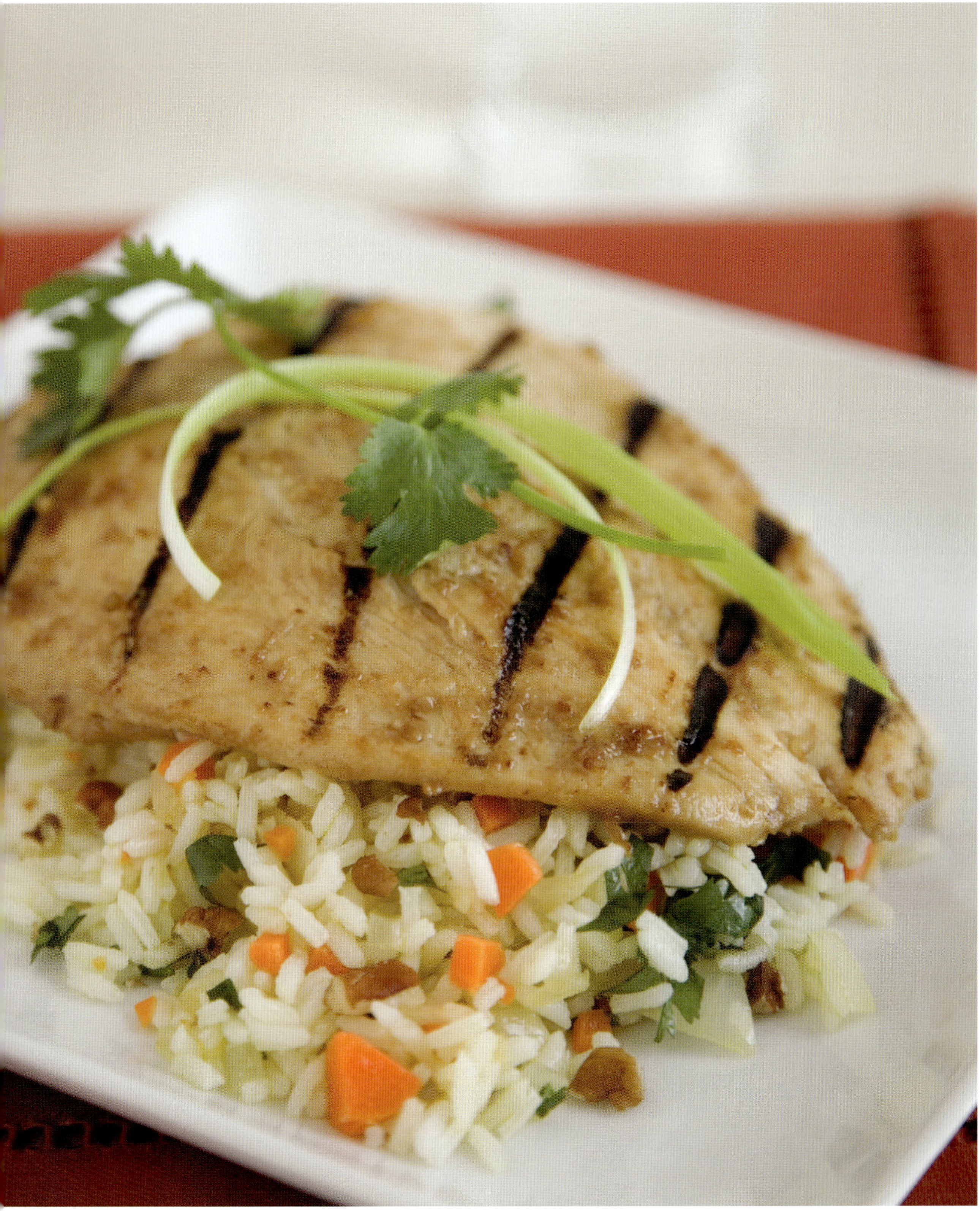

Pecan Rice Pilaf

Makes 4 servings

1½ tablespoons olive oil

½ cup finely chopped yellow onions

¼ cup chopped carrots

1 cup long-grain white rice

1½ cups chicken broth

Salt and white pepper to taste

¼ cup chopped toasted pecans

1 tablespoon chopped fresh cilantro

Heat the oil in a small saucepan over medium heat. Add the onions and carrots and cook, stirring, until the vegetables are slightly soft, 2 to 3 minutes.

Add the rice and chicken broth, and season with salt and pepper. Bring to a boil. Reduce the heat to medium low, cover, and simmer until the rice is tender and the broth is absorbed, about 20 minutes.

Remove from the heat and let stand for 5 minutes. Add the pecans and cilantro. Fluff with a fork before serving.

To serve, place equal portions of the pilaf in the center of 4 dinner plates, top with the chicken, and garnish with the green onions.

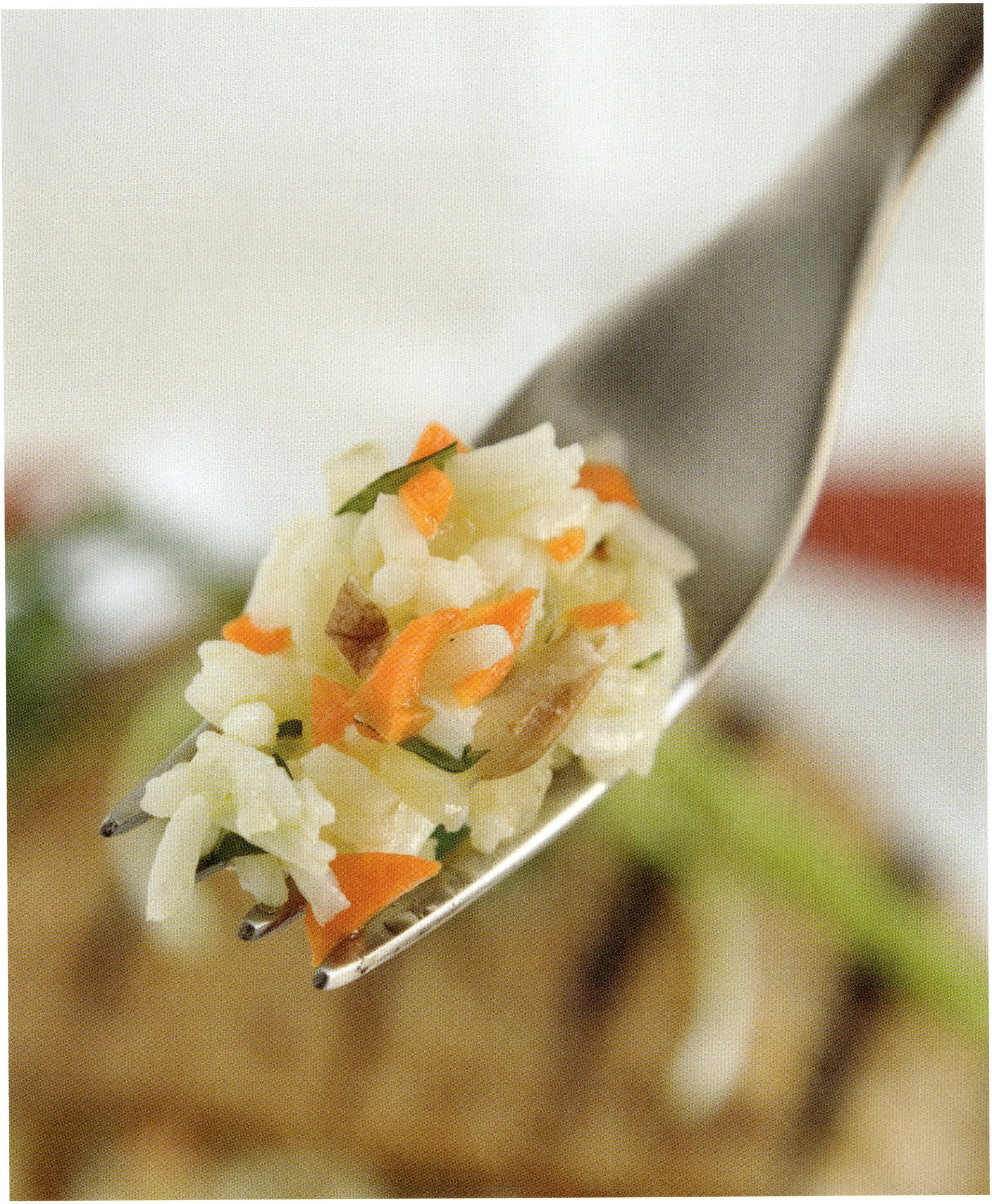

Lemon Chicken with Capers and Pecans and Super-Duper Yams

Quick and easy, this dish can be pulled together at the last minute. The sweetness of the yams rounds out the tartness of the lemon-butter sauce on the chicken. Add salad greens tossed with vinaigrette and you have a delightful dinner.

Makes 4 servings

¼ cup chopped pecans

4 chicken breasts (each 6 to 8 ounces), deboned and skinless

½ teaspoon salt

¼ teaspoon freshly ground black pepper

1 tablespoon olive oil

½ cup dry white wine

1½ tablespoons fresh lemon juice

1 tablespoon capers, drained

3 tablespoons unsalted butter

Chopped parsley for garnish (optional)

Spread the pecans on the bottom of a small skillet over medium heat. Cook, stirring, until golden brown, 2 to 3 minutes. Remove from the heat and set aside to cool.

Gently pound each chicken breast between two sheets of plastic wrap with a meat mallet until evenly flattened. Season with salt and pepper.

In a large skillet, heat the olive oil over medium-high heat, add the chicken breasts, and cook until golden brown, 3 to 4 minutes. Turn the breasts over and cook until the juices run clear, about 3 minutes.

Arrange the chicken on a large warmed platter. Cover loosely with foil to keep warm.

Pour off the fat from the skillet. Add the wine to the skillet and bring to a boil, scraping any brown bits from the bottom of the pan. Cook over high heat for 3 minutes.

Add the lemon juice and capers. Remove from the heat and whisk in the butter, 1 tablespoon at a time. To serve, pour the sauce over the chicken and sprinkle with the pecans. Garnish with parsley if you wish.

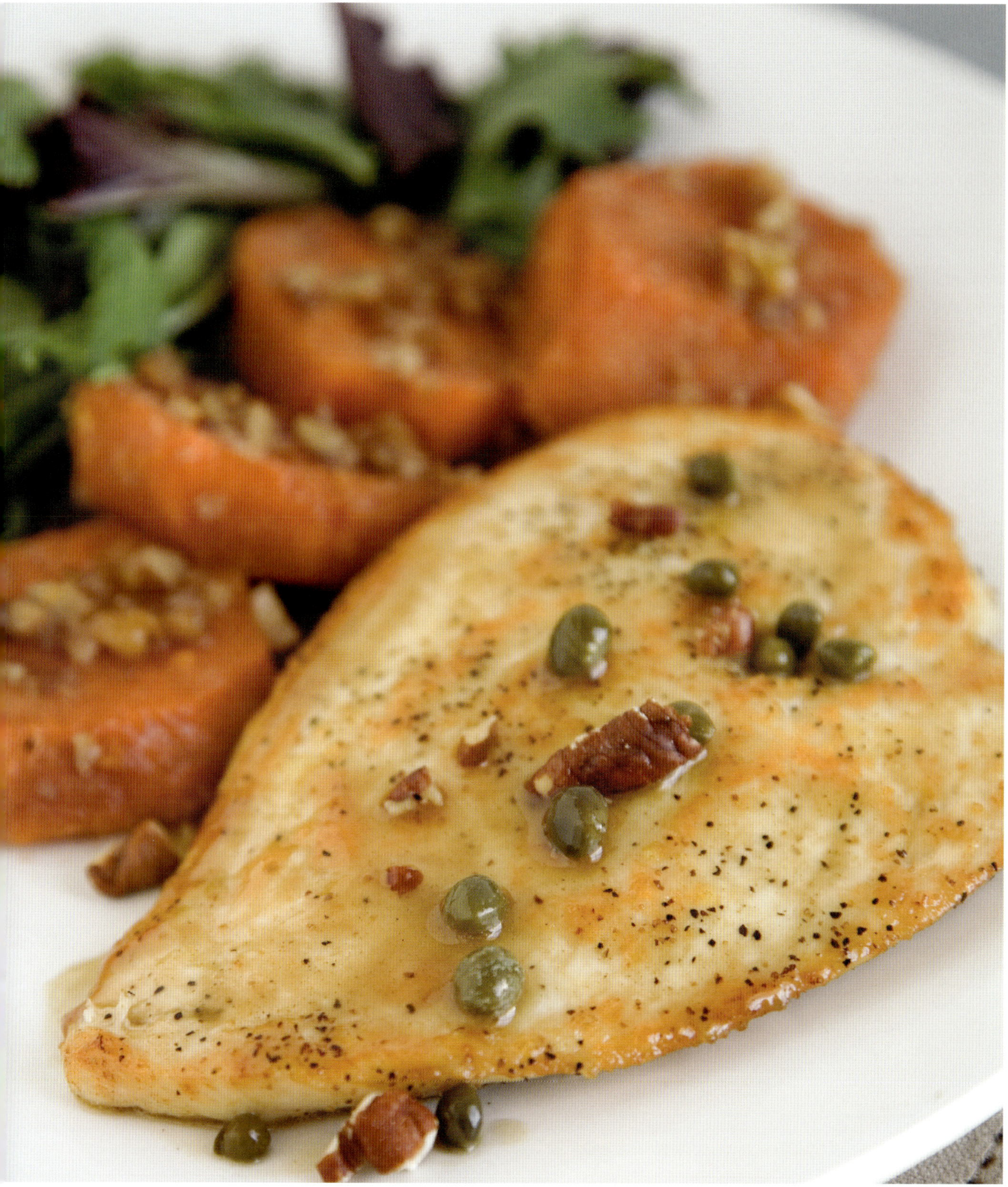

Super-Duper Yams

Makes 4 servings

4 medium-size sweet potatoes

¼ cup chopped pecans

3 tablespoons light brown sugar

1½ tablespoons butter

3 teaspoons dark crème de cacao

½ cup honey

Preheat the oven to 400 degrees.

Line a baking sheet with parchment paper and place the potatoes on the baking sheet. Bake for 30 minutes, then reduce the heat to 375 degrees and bake until soft to the touch, about 20 minutes.

Remove from the oven and cool. When cool enough to handle, remove the skins and slice the potatoes into ½-inch rounds. Arrange the potatoes in a baking dish large enough to accommodate the potatoes in 1 layer.

Increase the oven temperature to 425 degrees.

Sprinkle the potatoes with the pecans and brown sugar, dot with butter, and drizzle evenly with the crème de cacao and honey. Bake until heated through, about 15 minutes. Serve hot.

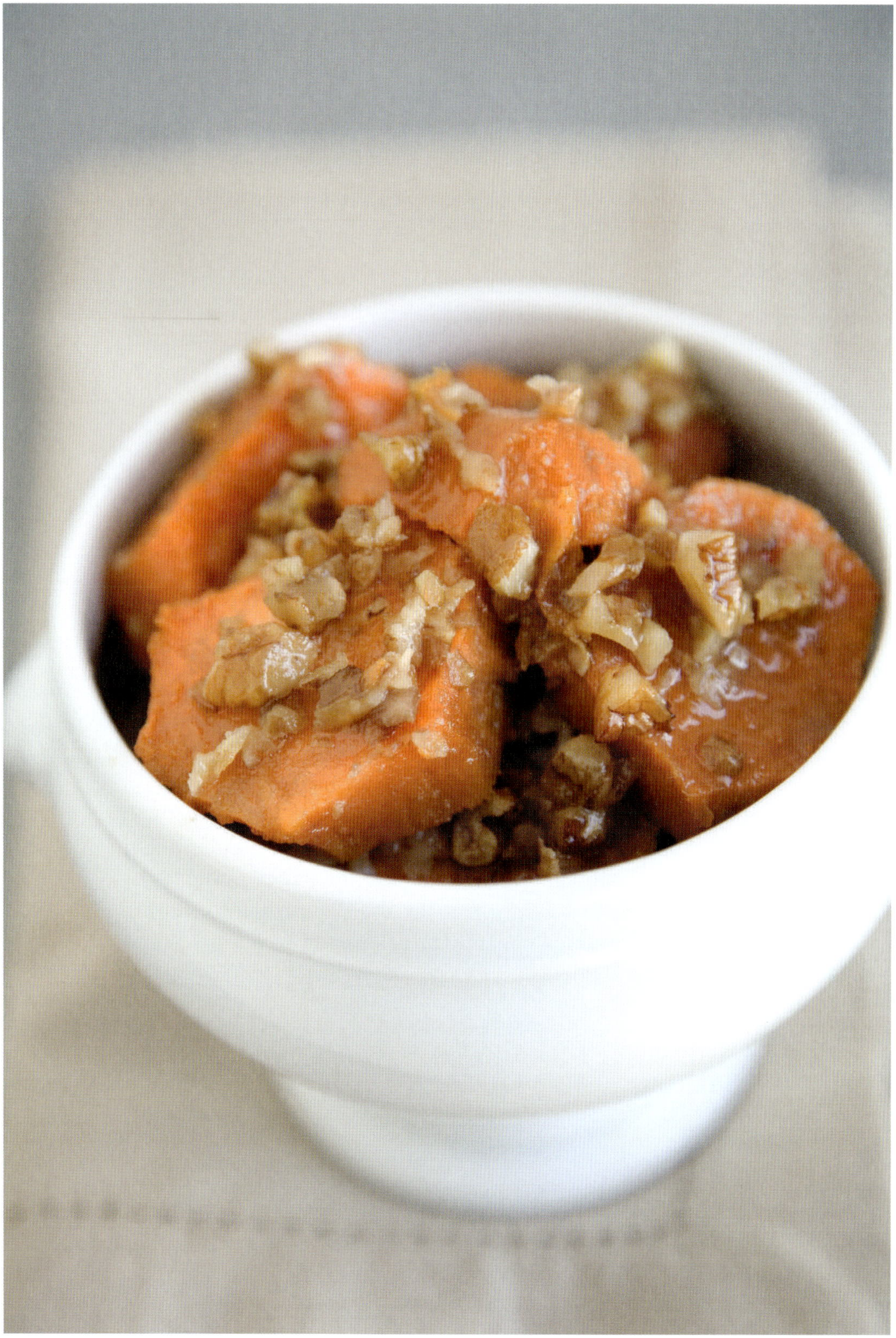

Broiled Redfish with Pecans and Chili-Roasted Sweet Potatoes

If you can't find redfish, use whatever fish is available in your area. The roasted sweet potatoes, flavored with cumin, chili powder, and paprika and tossed with pecans (roasted or not—your choice), complement the fish perfectly.

Makes 6 servings

2 tablespoons olive oil

6 redfish (or any firm, white-flesh fish) fillets (each about 8 ounces)

Salt, cayenne pepper, and hot sauce to taste

1 medium-size onion, thinly sliced

1 green bell pepper, thinly sliced

½ cup finely chopped celery

1 cup thinly sliced white button mushrooms

½ cup dry white wine

¼ cup fresh lemon juice

½ stick (4 tablespoons) butter, melted

1 cup pecan meal

Preheat the oven broiler. Arrange the oven rack about 4 inches from the heat. Oil the bottom of a baking pan with the olive oil and set aside.

Season the fillets with salt, cayenne, and hot sauce. Set aside.

Combine the onion, bell pepper, celery, and mushrooms in a mixing bowl. Season with salt, cayenne, and hot sauce and toss to mix. Arrange the vegetable mixture in 1 layer on the bottom of the prepared pan.

Arrange the fillets over the vegetables and sprinkle with ¼ cup of the wine and 2 tablespoons of the lemon juice. Put the pan under the broiler and cook for 2 to 3 minutes.

Remove from the oven and drizzle with the remaining wine and lemon juice, and add the butter. Sprinkle the pecan meal evenly over the fish. Return the pan to the oven and broil until the fish flakes easily with a fork, about 6 minutes longer.

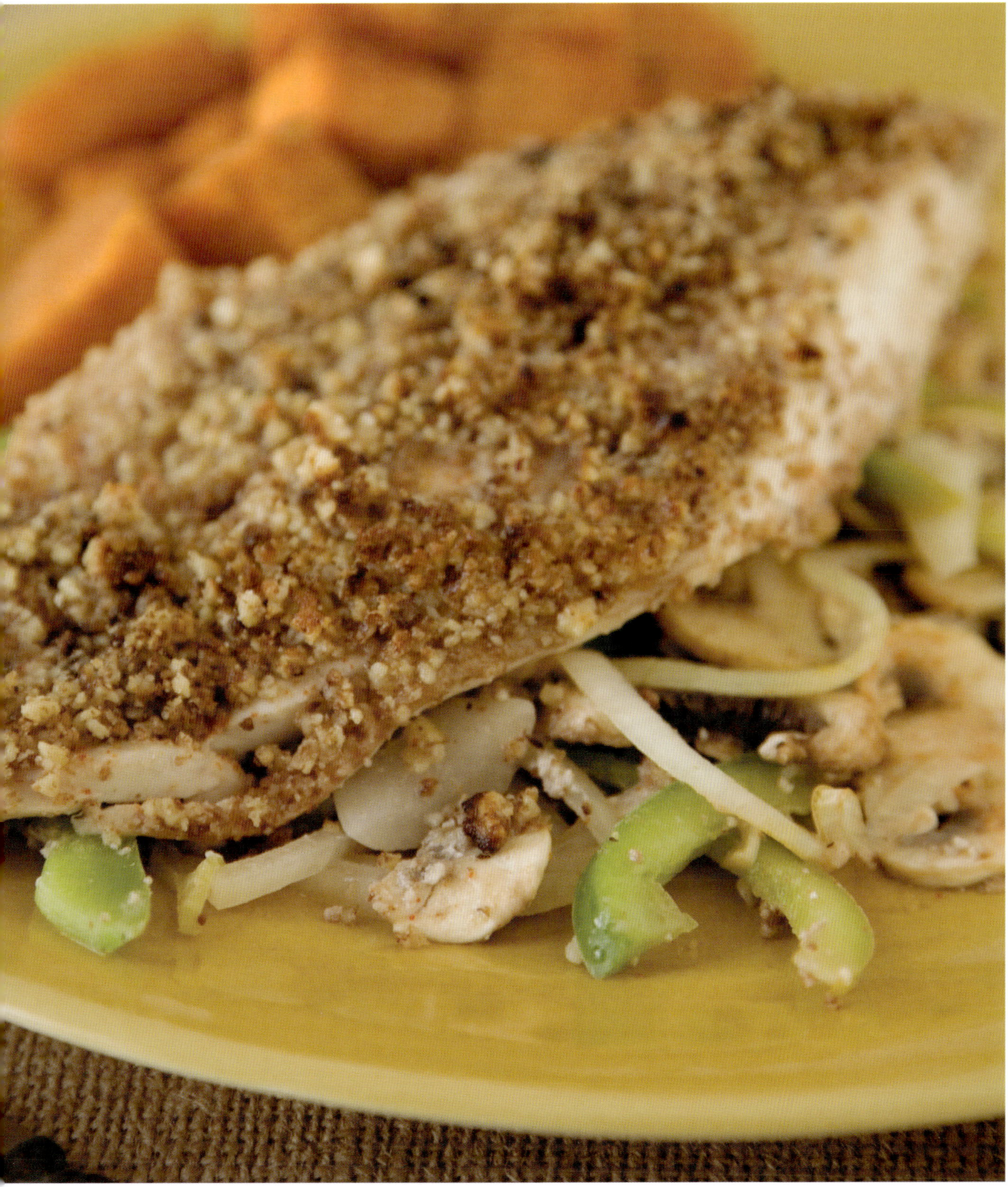

Chili-Roasted Sweet Potatoes

Makes 6 servings

6 medium-size sweet potatoes (uncooked)

2 teaspoons ground cumin

1 teaspoon chili powder

½ teaspoon sweet paprika

½ teaspoon salt

¼ teaspoon cayenne pepper

1½ tablespoons olive oil

¼ cup chopped pecans

Preheat the oven to 425 degrees. Peel the potatoes and cut into cubes.

Place the potatoes in a mixing bowl, add the dry seasonings, and toss to coat evenly. Drizzle with the olive oil and toss again to coat evenly. Arrange the potatoes in a single layer in a shallow baking pan lined with foil.

Roast on the lower rack for 8 minutes. Turn the potatoes over and roast until tender, 6 to 10 minutes. Remove from the oven and toss with the pecans. Serve warm.

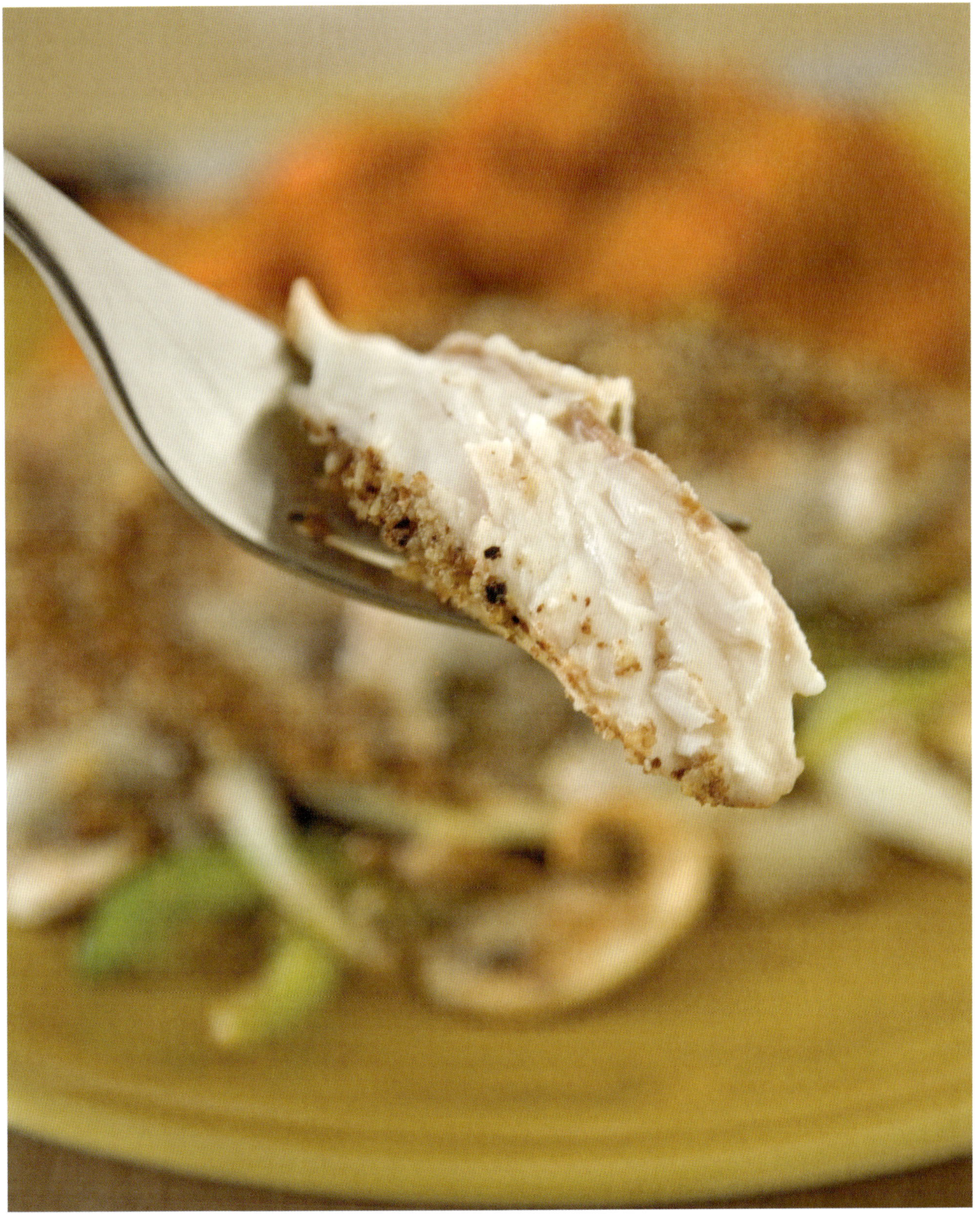

Speckled Trout with Pecan Meuniere, Green Beans, and Pecans

Much like trout amandine, a popular south Louisiana dish, the fish is pecan crusted to give it a wonderfully crispy texture and a delicious flavor.

Makes 6 servings

6 speckled trout (or other white, firm-fleshed fish) fillets (each about 8 ounces)

Salt and cayenne pepper to taste

¾ cup all-purpose flour

2 eggs, lightly beaten

¼ cup evaporated milk

½ stick (4 tablespoons) butter

3 tablespoons vegetable oil

2 cups roasted chopped pecans

1 tablespoon fresh lemon juice

2 tablespoons Worcestershire sauce

Preheat the boiler.

Season the fillets with salt and cayenne. Put the flour in a shallow bowl. Place the eggs and the milk in another shallow bowl and whisk to blend.

Dredge the fillets first in the flour, tapping off any excess, then in the egg mixture, allowing any excess to drip off.

Heat the butter and oil in a large nonstick skillet over medium-hot heat. Add the fish and fry until golden brown, about 3 minutes per side and transfer them to a baking sheet.

Combine 1½ cups of the pecans with the lemon juice, Worcestershire sauce, and the pan drippings in a food processor or an electric blender and process until the mixture is smooth.

Spread the mixture over the trout and place about 3 inches under the broiler to brown evenly, 1 to 2 minutes.

Remove from the oven and sprinkle with the remaining ½ cup pecans and serve.

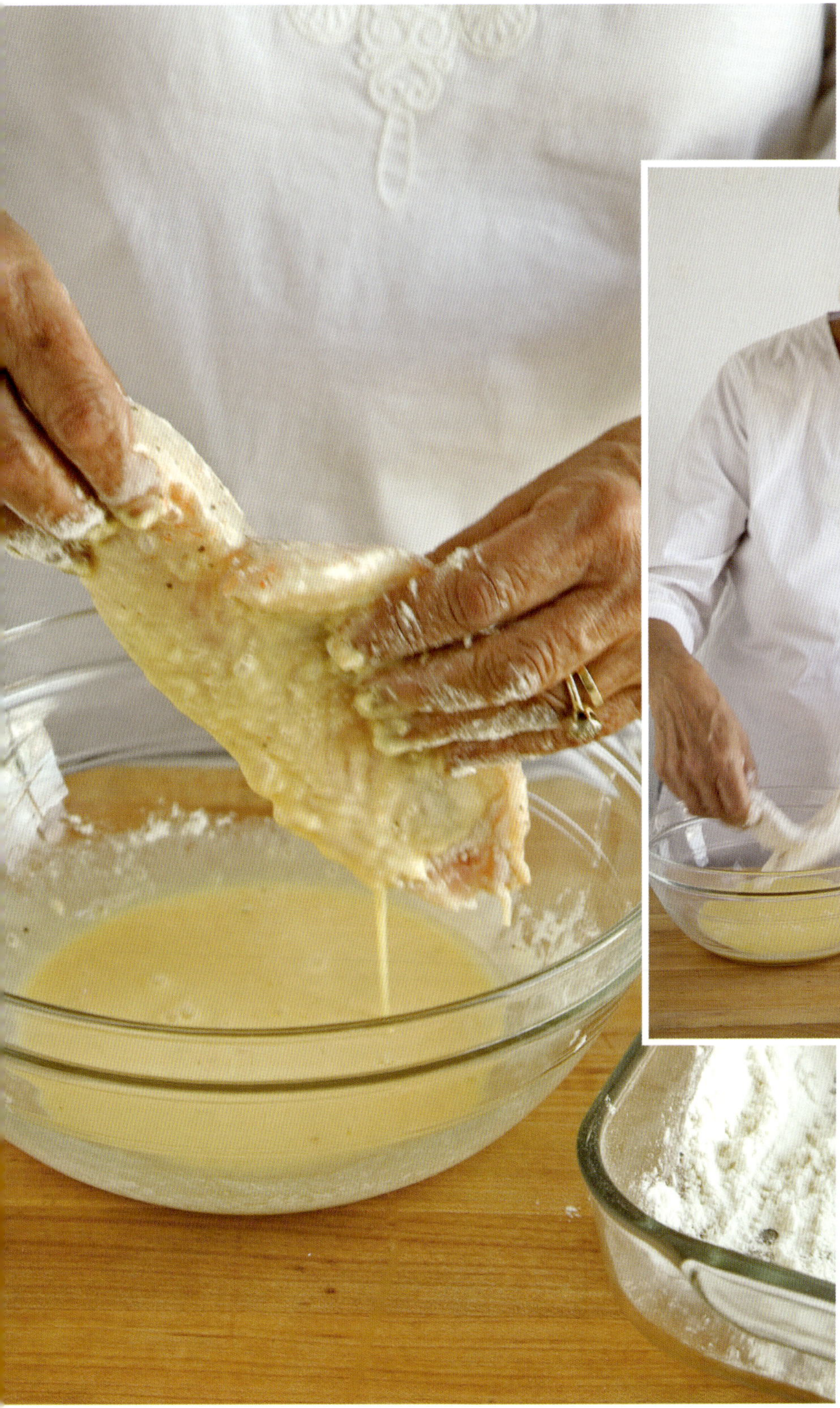

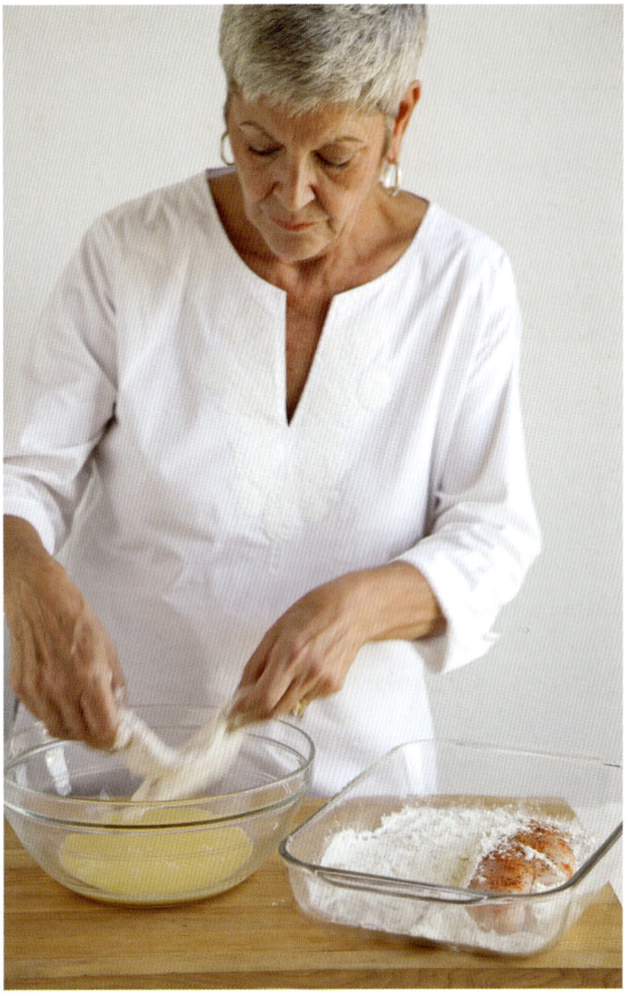

Green Beans and Pecans

Makes 6 servings

1¼ pound fresh green beans, trimmed

1 tablespoon olive oil

1 tablespoon butter

⅓ cup chopped pecans

3 tablespoons chopped pimentos, drained

¼ teaspoon salt

¼ teaspoon freshly ground black pepper

Bring a pot of salted water to a boil. Add the beans and cook until the beans are just tender, 3 to 5 minutes, depending on their size. Drain and transfer the beans to a bowl of cold water for 2 to 3 minutes. Drain and pat dry. Set aside.

Heat the olive oil and butter in a large saucepan over medium heat. Add the pecan pieces and cook, stirring, until the pecans are lightly toasted, about 2 minutes.

Add the beans and pimentos and season with salt and pepper. Toss gently to coat evenly. Serve warm.

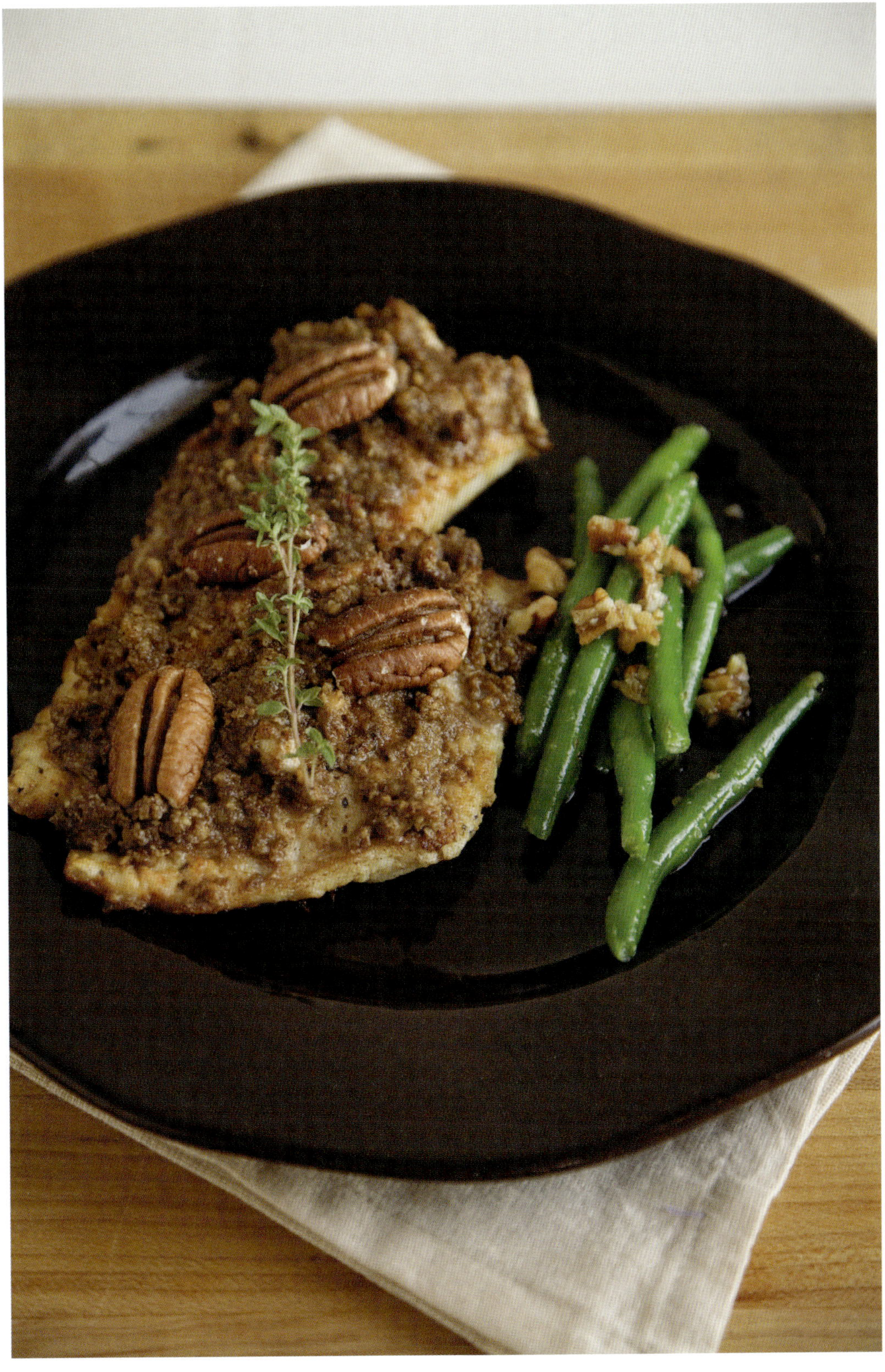

Pecan-Crusted Salmon with Pecan-Breaded Eggplant

Salmon is very delicate so be sure not to bake it too long or else it will become dry. You can also apply this preparation to tuna steaks.

If you prefer a crunchier finish to the coating on the salmon, place the fish under the broiler for about 30 seconds before serving.

For another use, try the breaded eggplant topped with fried shrimp or oysters.

Makes 4 servings

4 salmon fillets (each 6 to 7 ounces)

Salt and freshly ground black pepper to taste

2 tablespoons fresh lemon juice

1 tablespoon Creole mustard

1 cup dried fine breadcrumbs

¼ cup ground pecans

2 teaspoons olive oil

Preheat the oven to 375 degrees. Lightly oil a 9x13-inch baking dish.

Season the salmon fillets with salt and pepper and arrange in the prepared baking dish.

Combine the lemon juice, Creole mustard, breadcrumbs, and pecans in a small bowl and mix to blend. Spread an equal amount of the breadcrumb mixture on each fillet and pat gently. Drizzle olive oil over the breadcrumb mixture. Bake until the center of the salmon is just opaque and the crumb topping is golden, 12 to 15 minutes.

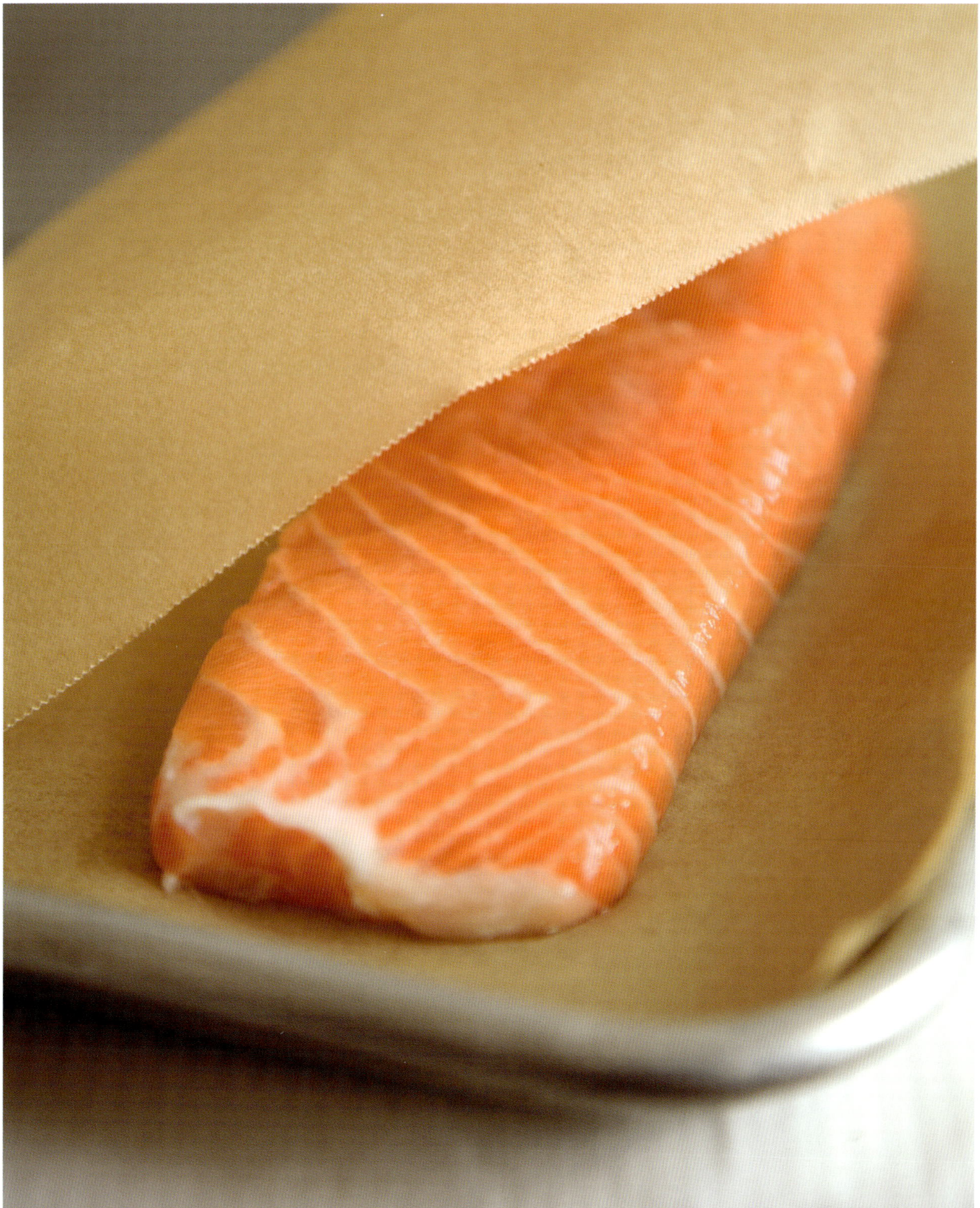

Pecan-Breaded Eggplant

Makes 4 servings

1 eggplant (about 1 pound)

Salt

2 eggs, lightly beaten

¾ cup all-purpose flour

¾ cup ground pecans

3 tablespoons freshly grated Parmesan cheese

1½ teaspoons sweet paprika

¾ teaspoon Italian seasoning

Salt and cayenne pepper to taste

½ cup vegetable oil (or more as needed)

Cut the eggplant into ¼-inch-thick slices. Put the eggplant slices in a large shallow dish and sprinkle generously with salt. Let stand for 30 minutes. Rinse the eggplant with cool tap water and pat dry.

Place the eggs in a shallow bowl. Combine the flour, pecans, cheese, paprika, and Italian seasoning in another shallow bowl and season with salt and cayenne.

Dredge the eggplant slices first in the eggs, letting the excess drip off, then dredge in the flour mixture, tapping off any excess.

Heat 2 tablespoons of the oil in a large, heavy skillet over medium heat. Fry 2 to 3 slices of the eggplant at a time until golden brown, about 1 minute per side, and drain on paper towels. Repeat the process with more oil and the remaining eggplant slices until all are cooked.

To serve, arrange equal amounts of the fried eggplant in the center of 4 dinner plates and top each serving with a salmon fillet.

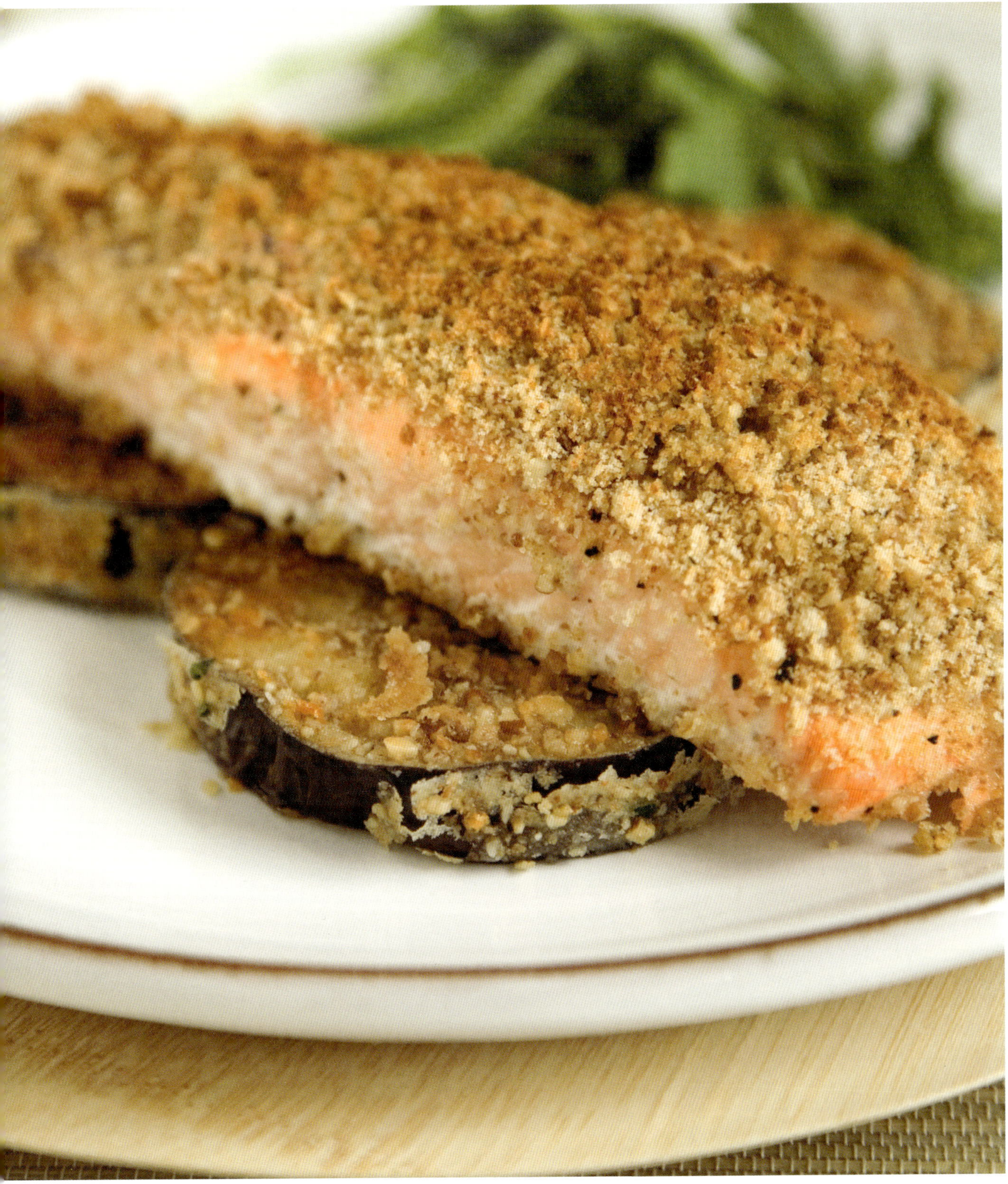

Crab Cakes with Pecan-Butter Sauce and Pecan Bread Dressing

Crab cakes are a popular Southern dish and are usually served with tartar sauce, but this pecan-butter sauce is a great alternative. The pecan bread dressing can also be served with roasted chicken or pork chops.

Makes 6 servings

½ stick (4 tablespoons) butter

½ cup finely chopped onions

½ cup finely chopped green bell peppers

½ cup mayonnaise

2 teaspoons Creole mustard

2 tablespoons finely chopped parsley

1 teaspoon salt

¼ teaspoon cayenne pepper

⅛ teaspoon hot sauce

1 teaspoon baking powder

1 egg, lightly beaten

2 cups finely crushed buttery crackers, such as Ritz or Escort

1 pound lump crabmeat, picked over for shells and cartilage

¼ cup vegetable oil (or more as needed)

Heat the butter in a large skillet over medium heat. Add the onions and bell peppers and cook, stirring, until soft and lightly golden, about 8 minutes. Remove from the heat and set aside to cool.

Combine the mayonnaise, mustard, parsley, salt, cayenne, hot sauce, baking powder, egg, 1 cup of the crushed crackers, and the crabmeat in a large mixing bowl. Add the onions and bell peppers and mix gently. Form the mixture into 6 plump cakes and refrigerate for at least 2 hours.

Remove the cakes from the refrigerator and dredge them in the remaining crushed crackers to coat evenly.

Heat the oil in a large skillet over medium heat. Add the crab cakes, 2 at a time, and fry until golden brown, 2 to 3 minutes on each side. Drain on paper towels. Serve warm drizzled with the butter sauce.

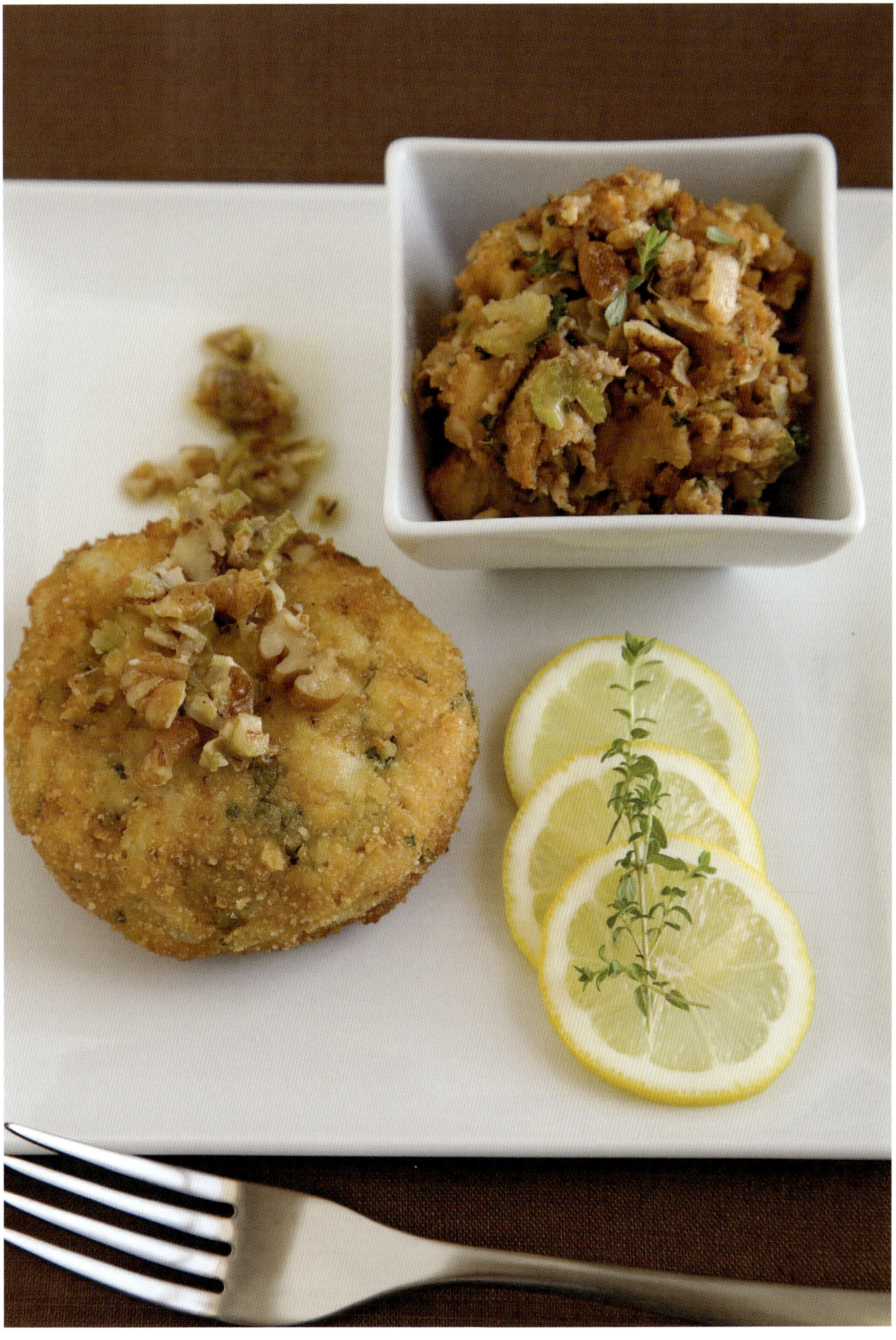

Pecan-Butter Sauce

Makes 4 servings

1 stick (8 tablespoons) butter

1 tablespoon chopped green onions (green part only)

1 garlic clove, crushed

½ teaspoon salt

⅛ teaspoon hot sauce

Pinch of dried marjoram leaves

2 tablespoons fresh lemon juice

¼ cup chopped pecans

Melt the butter in a small saucepan over medium heat. Add the green onions and the garlic and cook, stirring, for 1 minute. Add the salt, hot sauce, marjoram, lemon juice, and pecans, and cook, whisking, for 2 minutes. Remove from the heat and serve immediately.

Pecan Bread Dressing

Preheat the oven to 350 degrees. Butter a 9x13-inch casserole and set aside.

Cook the sausage in a small skillet until completely browned. Remove from the heat and drain on paper towels. Set aside.

Melt the butter in a medium-size skillet over medium heat. Add the onions, celery, and garlic and cook, stirring, until soft, 4 to 5 minutes. Remove from the heat and transfer the mixture to a large bowl. Add the sausage, bread, parsley, green onions, thyme, and pecans. Season with salt and cayenne. Mix well. Add enough broth to moisten the mixture.

Transfer the mixture to the prepared pan and bake until warmed through, about 30 minutes.

Makes 6 to 8 servings

¼ pound fresh pork sausage, removed from the casing and crumbled

6 tablespoons butter

½ cup chopped yellow onions

¾ cup chopped celery

2 garlic cloves, crushed

4 cups cubed day-old French bread

¼ cup chopped parsley

¼ cup chopped green onions (green part only)

¼ teaspoon dried thyme leaves

1 cup coarsely chopped pecans

1 teaspoon salt

¼ teaspoon cayenne pepper

½ cup chicken broth (or more as needed)

Crabmeat Royale with Pecans and Broccoli with Caramelized Shallots

Fresh, sweet lump crabmeat needs little enhancements save for butter, lemon juice, herbs, spices, and, of course, pecans. This is a delightful meal to serve on a warm summer evening. As an alternative to the broccoli, serve vine-ripened tomatoes drizzled with olive oil and splashed with balsamic vinegar.

Makes 4 servings

1 stick (8 tablespoons) butter, melted

2 pounds jumbo lump crabmeat, picked over for shells and cartilage

2 tablespoons fresh lemon juice

1 tablespoon finely chopped green onions (green part only)

1 tablespoon minced parsley

Salt and freshly ground black pepper to taste

3 tablespoons roasted chopped pecans

Preheat the oven to 325 degrees.

Gently toss the butter with the crabmeat in a mixing bowl. Add the lemon juice, green onions, and parsley and season with salt and pepper. Gently toss again to mix.

Mound the mixture equally into 4 ramekins and sprinkle with the pecans. Bake until just warmed through, 10 to 12 minutes.

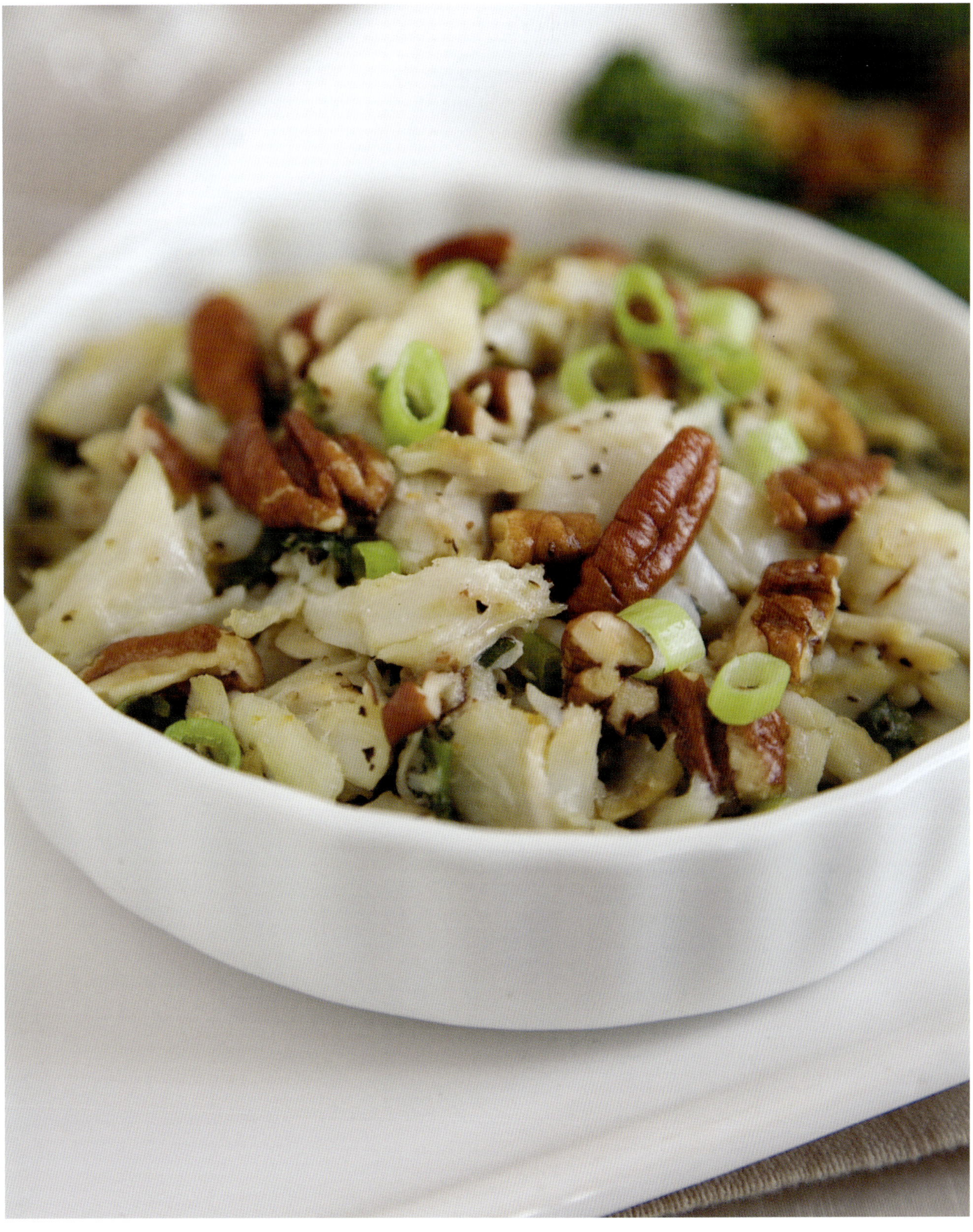

Broccoli with Caramelized Shallots

Makes 4 servings

1½ teaspoons olive oil

1 tablespoon butter

4 large shallots, thinly sliced

Salt and freshly ground black pepper to taste

1 bunch broccoli (about 1½ pounds), cut into florets

1 tablespoon roasted chopped pecans

Heat the oil and butter in a large nonstick skillet over medium-low heat. Add the shallots and cook, stirring often, to a deep golden brown, about 10 minutes. Season with salt and pepper and set aside.

Cook the broccoli in boiling, salted water until just tender, 3 to 5 minutes. Drain and add to the shallots in the skillet. Gently toss. Adjust seasoning if necessary. Sprinkle with the pecans and serve warm.

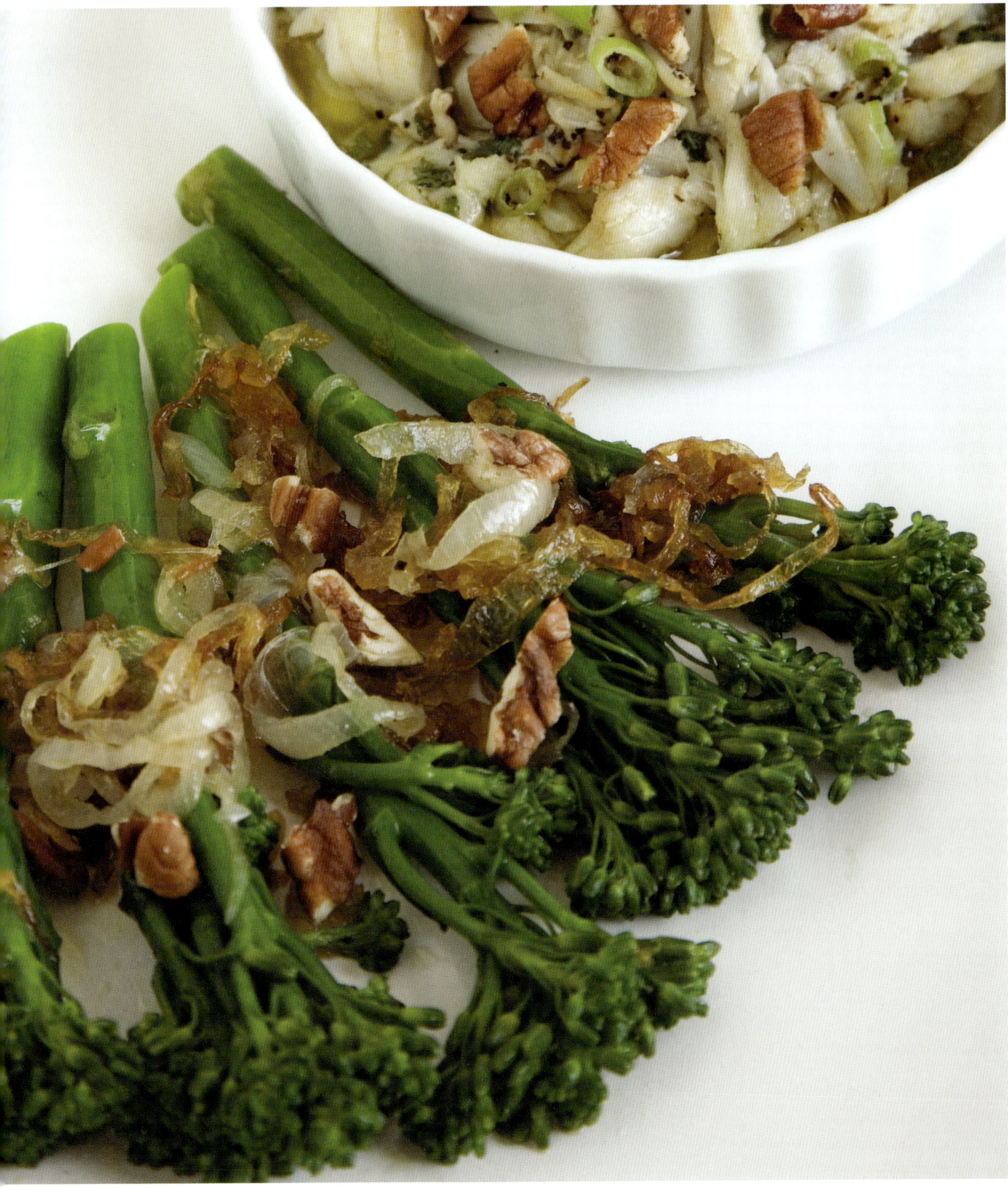

Shrimp, Vegetable, and Pecan Pasta

Shrimp tossed with vegetables and pasta is always a delicious treat. Wonderful for an informal meal on the patio or by the pool, this dish is given added flavor by the pecans. If you don't have shrimp, try this recipe with scallops.

Makes 6 servings

2 tablespoons butter

2 tablespoons olive oil

1 medium-size red bell pepper, cut into thin strips

1 medium-size green bell pepper, cut into thin strips

2 shallots, chopped

1 tablespoon minced garlic

36 large shrimp, peeled and deveined

½ cup shrimp or chicken stock

⅔ cup heavy cream

1 pound angel hair pasta, cooked and drained

1 cup chopped fresh basil leaves (optional)

1 teaspoon salt

½ teaspoon freshly ground black pepper

¼ teaspoon cayenne pepper

½ cup chopped pecans

½ cup freshly grated Parmesan cheese

Melt the butter with the olive oil in a large skillet over medium-high heat. Add the bell peppers and shallots and cook, stirring, until the vegetables are just soft, about 3 minutes. Add the garlic and cook, stirring, for 1 minute. Using a slotted spoon, transfer the vegetables to a large bowl.

Add the shrimp to the hot skillet and cook, stirring, for 1 minute. Add the shrimp or chicken stock, scraping the bottom and sides of the skillet, and cook for 30 seconds. Add the cream and bring to a boil. Cook, stirring, until the shrimp are just cooked through, 3 to 4 minutes. Using a slotted spoon, remove the shrimp and place them in the bowl with the vegetables.

Boil the liquid in the skillet until it is reduced and thick enough to coat the back of a spoon, about 3 minutes. Pour the mixture into the bowl with the vegetables and shrimp. Add the pasta, basil, salt, black pepper, and cayenne. Toss to coat evenly.

Put equal amounts of the pasta mixture in shallow soup bowls and garnish with equal amounts of the pecan pieces and Parmesan cheese. Serve warm.

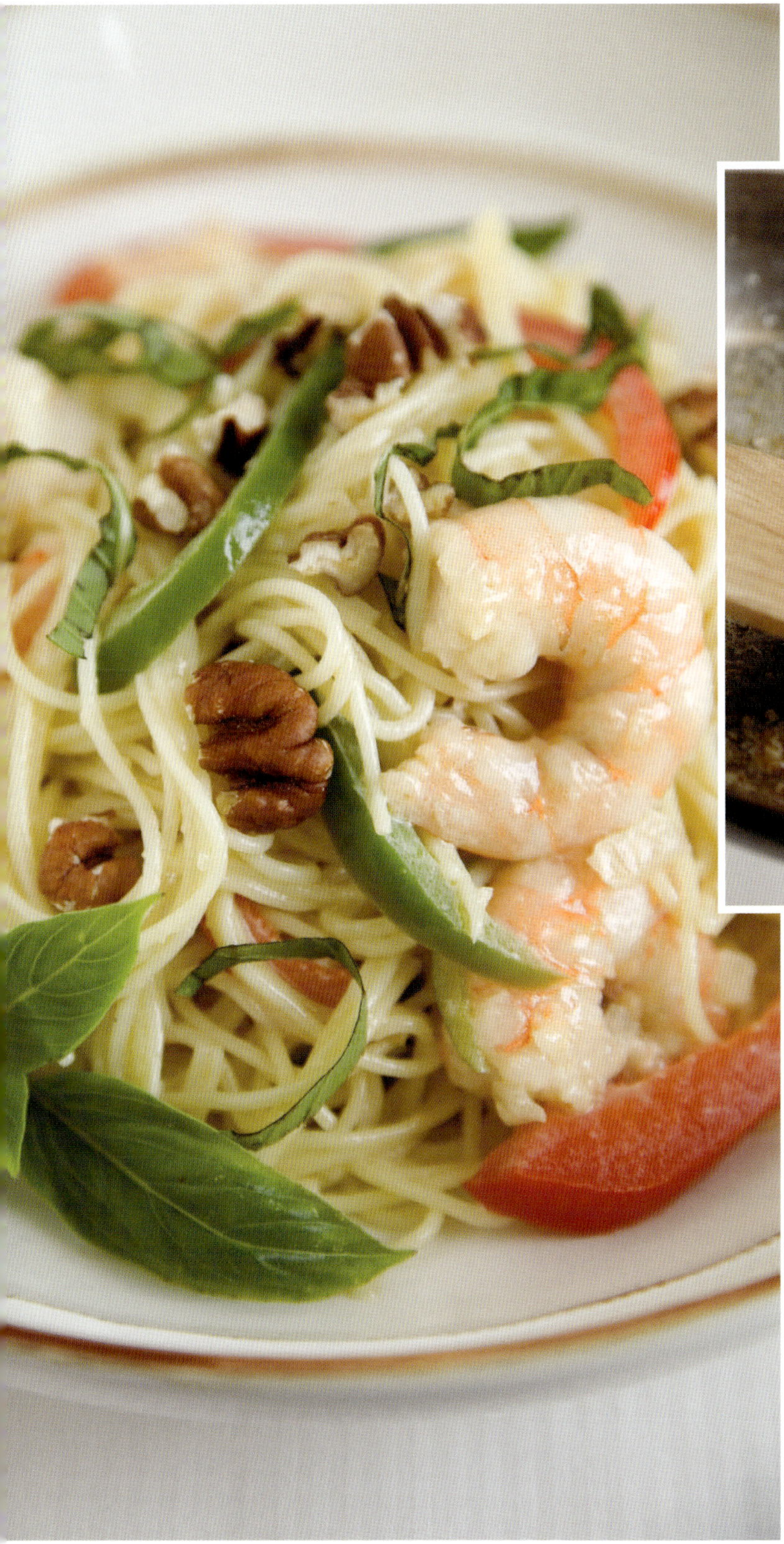
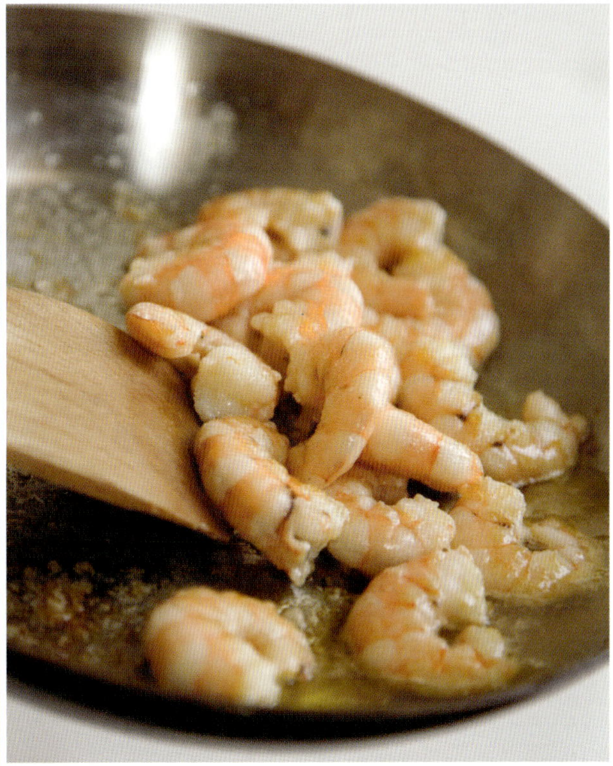

Stuffed Pork Chops with Asparagus and Pecan Butter

Thick-cut pork chops stuffed with dressing make a great main course for a casual dinner party. Asparagus bathed in pecan butter rounds out the meal.

Makes 6 servings

6 center-cut pork chops (each about 1½ inches thick)

5 tablespoons olive oil

½ cup finely chopped onions

½ cup finely chopped celery

2 tablespoons finely chopped tasso or smoked ham

¼ cup chopped pecan

2 slices of day-old bread, cut into 1-inch cubes

¼ cup beef broth

Salt, freshly ground black pepper, and cayenne pepper to taste

1 large egg, beaten

Italian-style breadcrumbs

Preheat the oven to 350 degrees.

With a sharp pointed knife, cut a pocket in each chop. Set aside.

Heat 3 tablespoons of the oil in a large skillet over medium heat. Add the onions, celery, tasso, and pecans, and cook, stirring, until the vegetables are soft, about 5 minutes. Remove from the heat.

In another skillet, heat the remaining 2 tablespoons of olive oil and add the cubed bread. Cook, stirring, until lightly browned, 2 to 3 minutes. Remove the bread from the skillet and drain on paper towels. Transfer to a mixing bowl.

Add the beef broth to the onion and tasso mixture and season with salt, black pepper, and cayenne. Stir the mixture together and pour over the croutons in the bowl. Toss to mix.

Divide the stuffing into six portions and stuff into the pockets of the pork chops. Close the pockets and secure with toothpicks.

Put the egg in a shallow bowl. Add the breadcrumbs to another shallow bowl. Dip the chops in the beaten egg, then dredge them in the breadcrumbs.

Place the chops in a lightly oiled shallow baking pan and cover them loosely with aluminum foil. Bake for 1 hour, turn the chops over and continue baking until the juices run clear, 20 to 30 minutes longer. Serve warm.

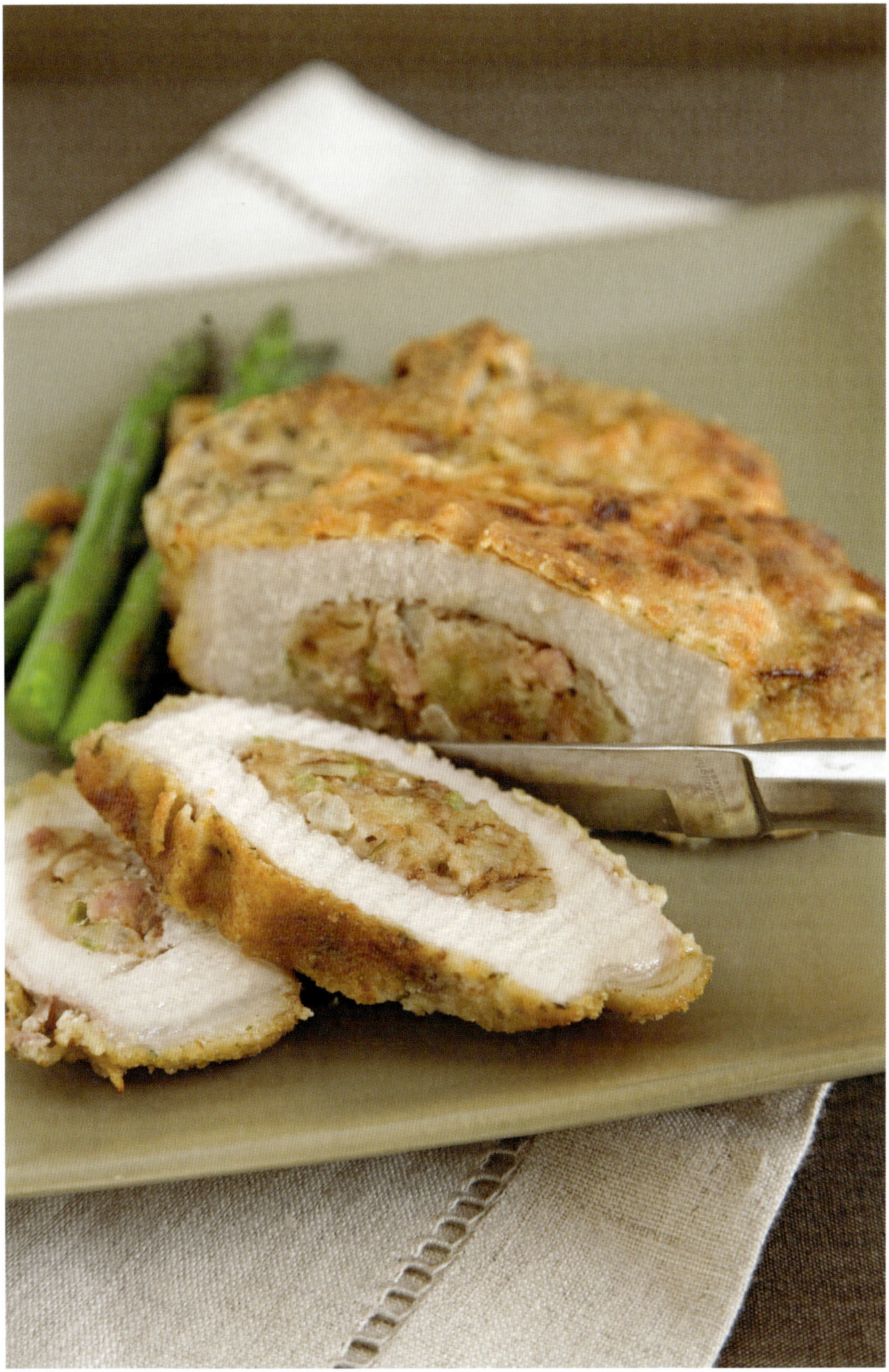

Asparagus and Pecan Butter

Makes 6 servings

2 cups water

1 teaspoon salt

2 pounds fresh asparagus, trimmed

6 tablespoons butter

2 tablespoons fresh lemon juice

2 tablespoons fresh orange juice

Salt and freshly ground black pepper to taste

¼ cup coarsely chopped pecans

Lemon zest for garnish

Combine the water and salt in a skillet and bring to a boil. Add the asparagus and cook until they are tender, 2 to 3 minutes. Remove from the heat, drain, and cool in an ice-water bath. Drain and pat dry with paper towels.

Melt the butter in a skillet over medium heat. Add the lemon juice and orange juice and whisk to blend. Cook, whisking constantly, for 2 minutes. Season with salt and pepper.

Arrange the asparagus on a serving platter and drizzle with the sauce. Garnish with the pecans and lemon zest. Serve immediately.

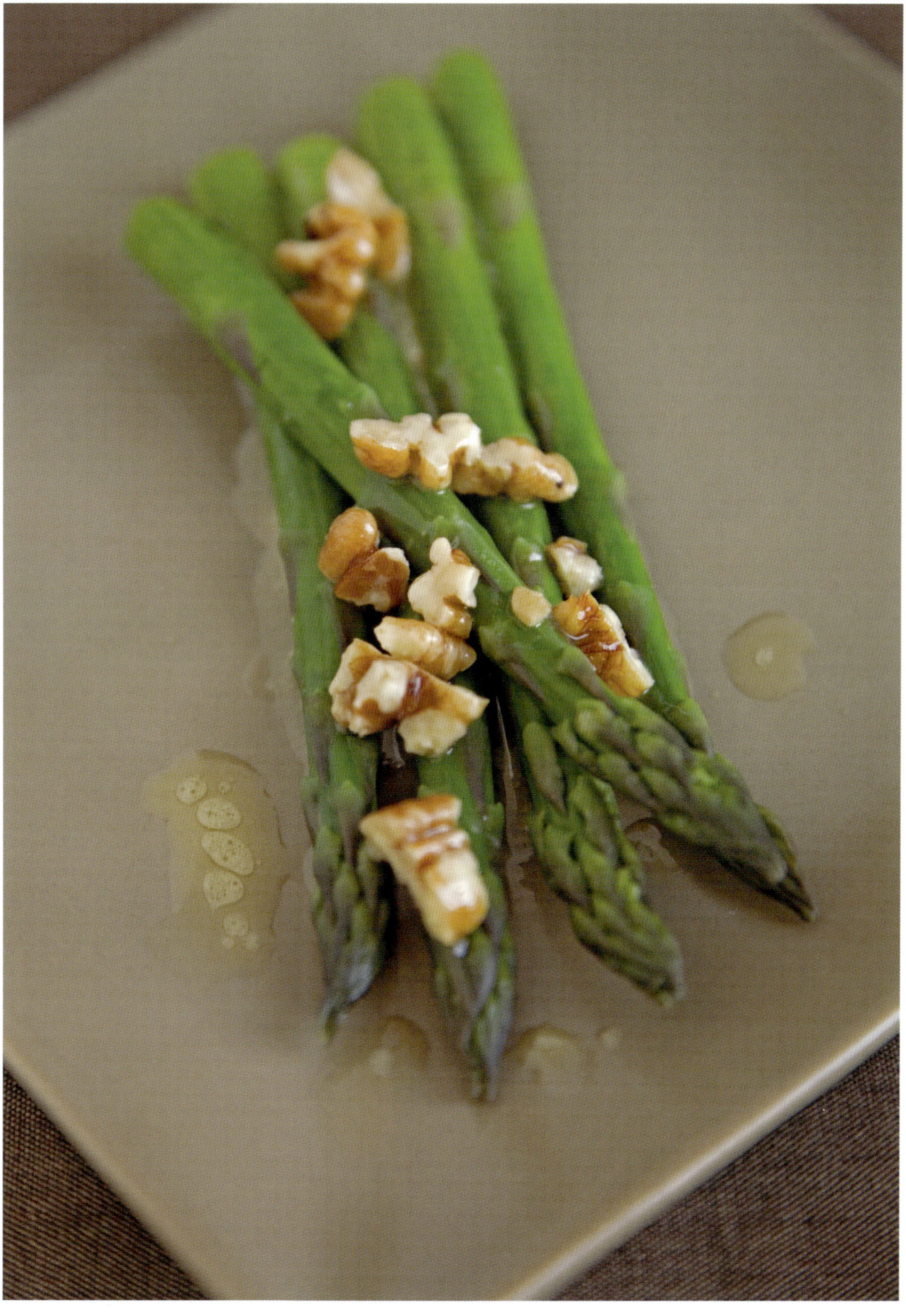

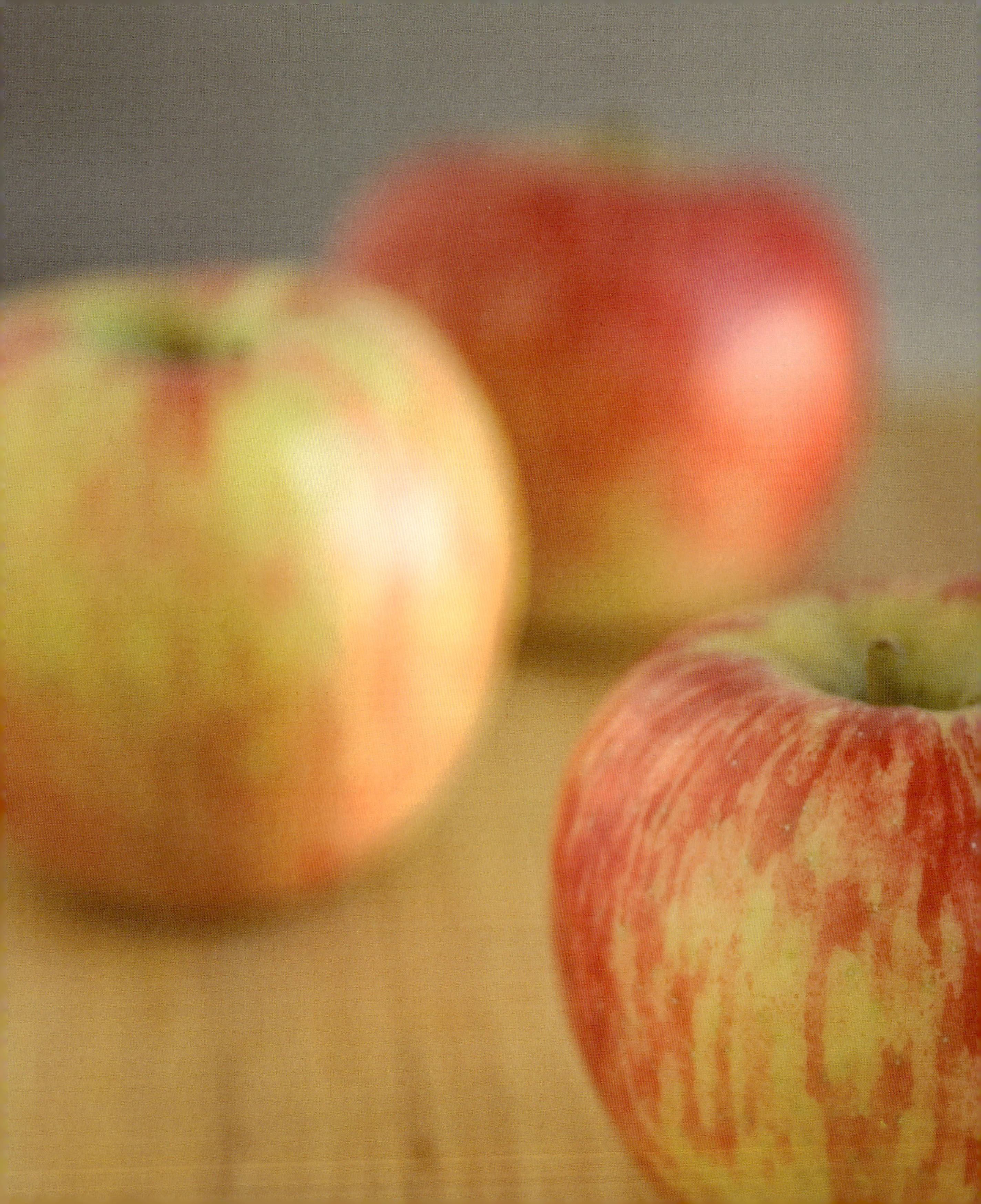

Chapter 5
Sweets for the Sweet

There are countless recipes for cakes, candies, pies, and cookies that incorporate pecans, and they never fail to please the palate. These sweet-delight recipes represent only a small collection of our favorites. Be creative and experiment. If you have a recipe that calls for other nuts, don't be afraid to substitute pecans. If you want an added depth of flavor, roast or toast the pecans before adding them to the recipe.

Apple Crisp

During the fall when apples are at their peak, this is a delightful dessert to serve warm from the oven and topped with a scoop or two of ice cream or a dollop of sweet whipped cream. The aroma as it bakes will fill the house with a delightful fragrance.

Makes 6 to 8 servings

1 cup all-purpose flour

1 cup oatmeal

½ teaspoon baking soda

1 teaspoon ground cinnamon

¼ teaspoon ground nutmeg

1 cup firmly packed brown sugar

1 stick (8 tablespoons) butter, melted

½ cup chopped pecans

5 medium-size sweet red apples, peeled, cored, and sliced

2 teaspoons fresh lemon juice

Vanilla ice cream or whipped cream for serving

Preheat the oven to 350 degrees. Lightly grease a 7x11-inch baking dish and set aside.

Combine the flour, oatmeal, baking soda, cinnamon, nutmeg, brown sugar, butter, and pecans in a large mixing bowl and mix well to blend.

Toss the apples with the lemon juice to coat evenly. Arrange the apples in the prepared pan and cover with the crumble mixture.

Bake until the crust is golden brown, 30 to 40 minutes. Remove from the oven and cool for a few minutes before serving with ice cream or whipped cream.

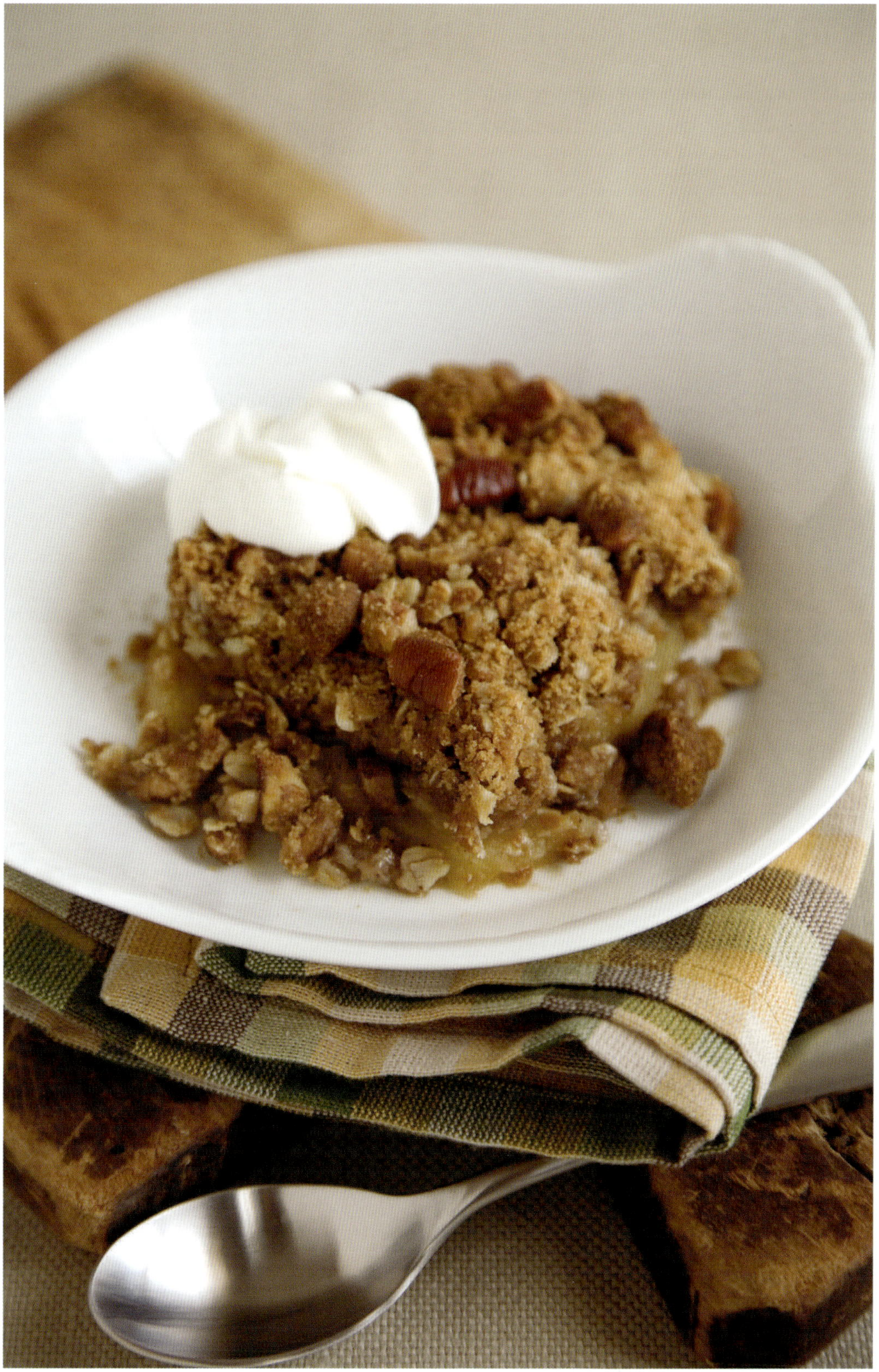

Banana Bourbon Cake

Make the cake and the crème anglaise ahead of time and bring it out for dessert to serve with coffee after a meal. If you don't care for bourbon, substitute rum or brandy. You can also experiment with rum extract.

This is an ideal dessert to serve during the summer following a barbecue or to bring along to a potluck supper.

Makes 12 servings

1½ cups chopped pecans

1½ cups raisins

3 cups all-purpose flour

3 teaspoons baking powder

1 teaspoon ground cinnamon

1 teaspoon ground ginger

½ teaspoon ground nutmeg

2 sticks (½ pound) butter, softened

2 cups sugar

3 ripe bananas, mashed

4 eggs

¾ cup bourbon

Crème Anglaise (recipe follows)

Preheat the oven to 350 degrees.

Toss the pecans and raisins in ½ cup of the flour and set aside.

Sift the remaining flour, the baking powder, cinnamon, ginger, and nutmeg together and set aside.

Combine the butter and sugar in a mixing bowl and beat with an electric mixer until light and fluffy. Add the bananas and beat until incorporated.

Add the eggs, one at a time, beating well after each addition.

Fold in the sifted flour mixture and the bourbon alternately, beginning and ending with the dry ingredients. Fold in the pecan-raisin mixture.

Spread the batter evenly into a greased 10-inch tube pan or Bundt pan.

Bake until a cake tester inserted in the cake comes out clean, about 1 hour and 15 minutes. Cool and remove from the pan.

Cut the cake into slices and serve each slice with a spoonful of the Crème Anglaise.

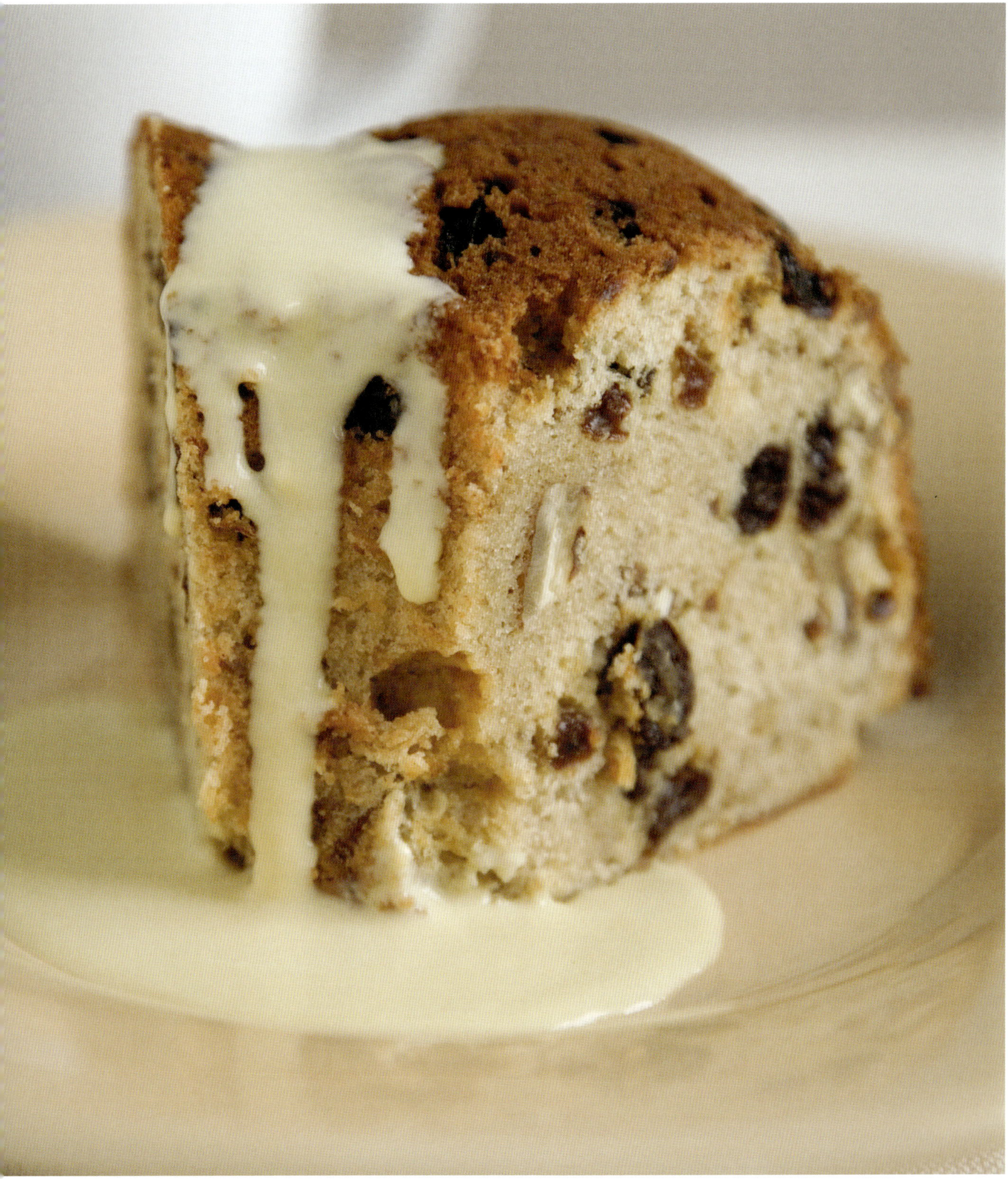

Crème Anglaise

1½ cups heavy cream

1 tablespoon light brown sugar

6 egg yolks

6 tablespoons maple syrup

6 tablespoons bourbon

Heat the cream and sugar in a small saucepan over medium heat and stir until the sugar dissolves. Remove from the heat.

Whisk the egg yolks together in a mixing bowl. Slowly beat in a third of the cream mixture, then whisk the egg yolk mixture back into the cream mixture.

Cook over low heat, stirring constantly, until it thickens enough to coat the back of a spoon. Be careful not to let the mixture boil.

Transfer to a clean bowl. Stir in the syrup and bourbon and cool. Store in an airtight container in the refrigerator until ready to use.

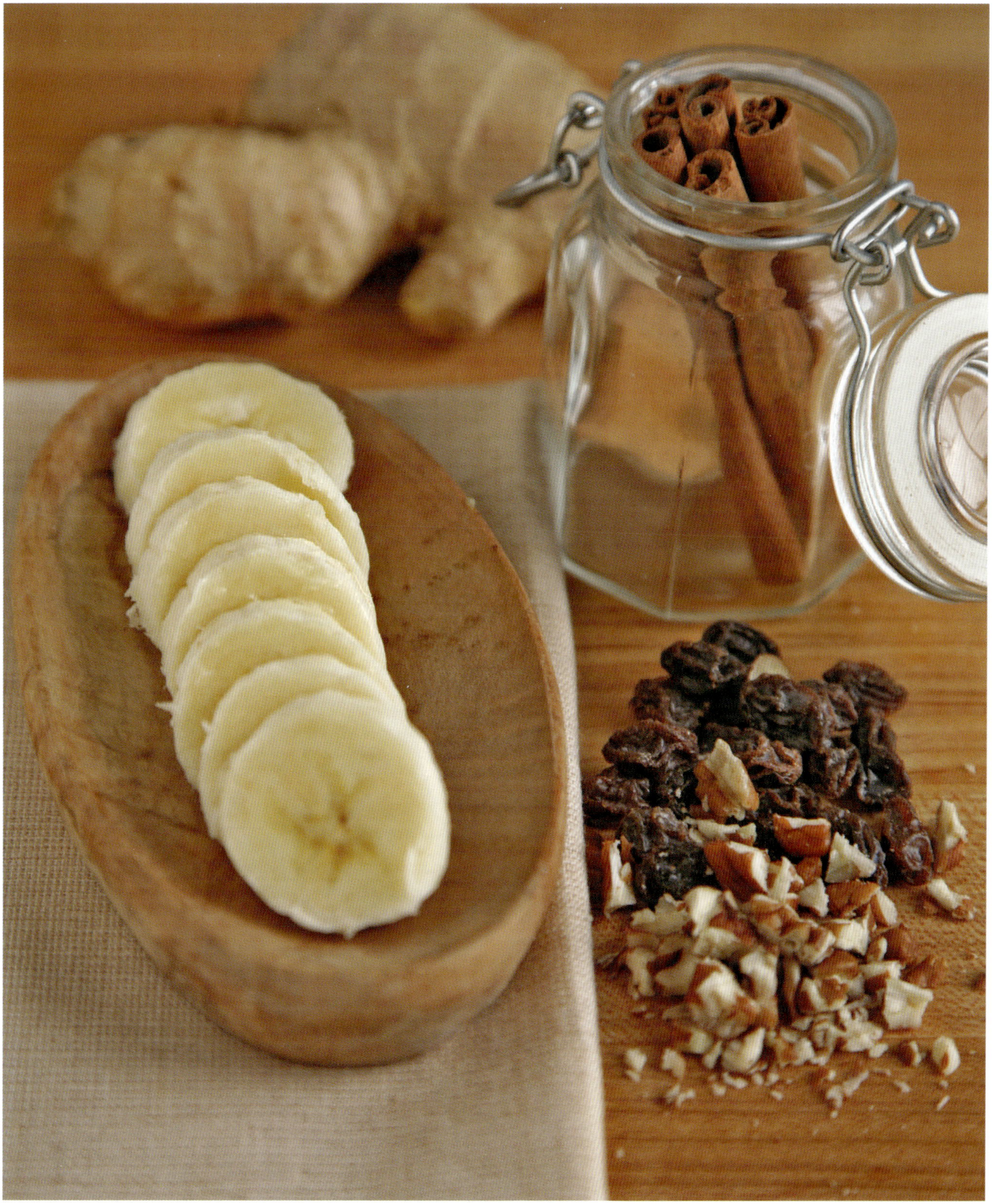

Banana Split Pie

As you can see, this is not a pie in the strict sense of the term. This pie is made in a large baking dish, making it an ideal dessert to prepare for family gatherings or potluck meals especially during the warm summer months. The graham cracker and pecan crust is layered with a creamy custard, then generously topped with sour cream, bananas, pineapples, cherries, whipped cream, and more pecans.

Makes 12 to 16 servings

1 cup pecan halves

2 cups graham cracker crumbs

1 stick (8 tablespoons) butter, melted

8 ounces cream cheese, softened

1 cup sugar

3 eggs

1 pint sour cream

5 ripe bananas, cut crosswise into ½-inch slices

1 15½-ounce can crushed pineapple, well drained

½ pint heavy cream, beaten until soft peaks form

1 cup chopped pecans

1 16-ounce jar maraschino cherries, drained and chopped

Preheat the oven to 325 degrees.

Put the pecan halves in a food processor or an electric blender and process to make a fine pecan meal.

Combine the graham cracker crumbs, pecan meal, and butter in a mixing bowl and mix well. Press the mixture onto the bottom and slightly up the sides of a 9x13-inch baking dish.

Combine the cream cheese and sugar in another mixing bowl and beat with an electric mixer until light and fluffy. Add the eggs, one at a time, beating well after each addition, until completely blended.

Spread this mixture evenly over the graham cracker crust and bake for 30 minutes.

Remove from the oven, spread the sour cream over the cream cheese mixture, and bake for 15 minutes longer. Remove from the oven and cool completely.

When cool, layer the bananas over the sour cream, spread on the pineapples, and then spread the whipped cream evenly over the top. Sprinkle with the chopped pecans and the cherries. Refrigerate for at least 2 hours before serving.

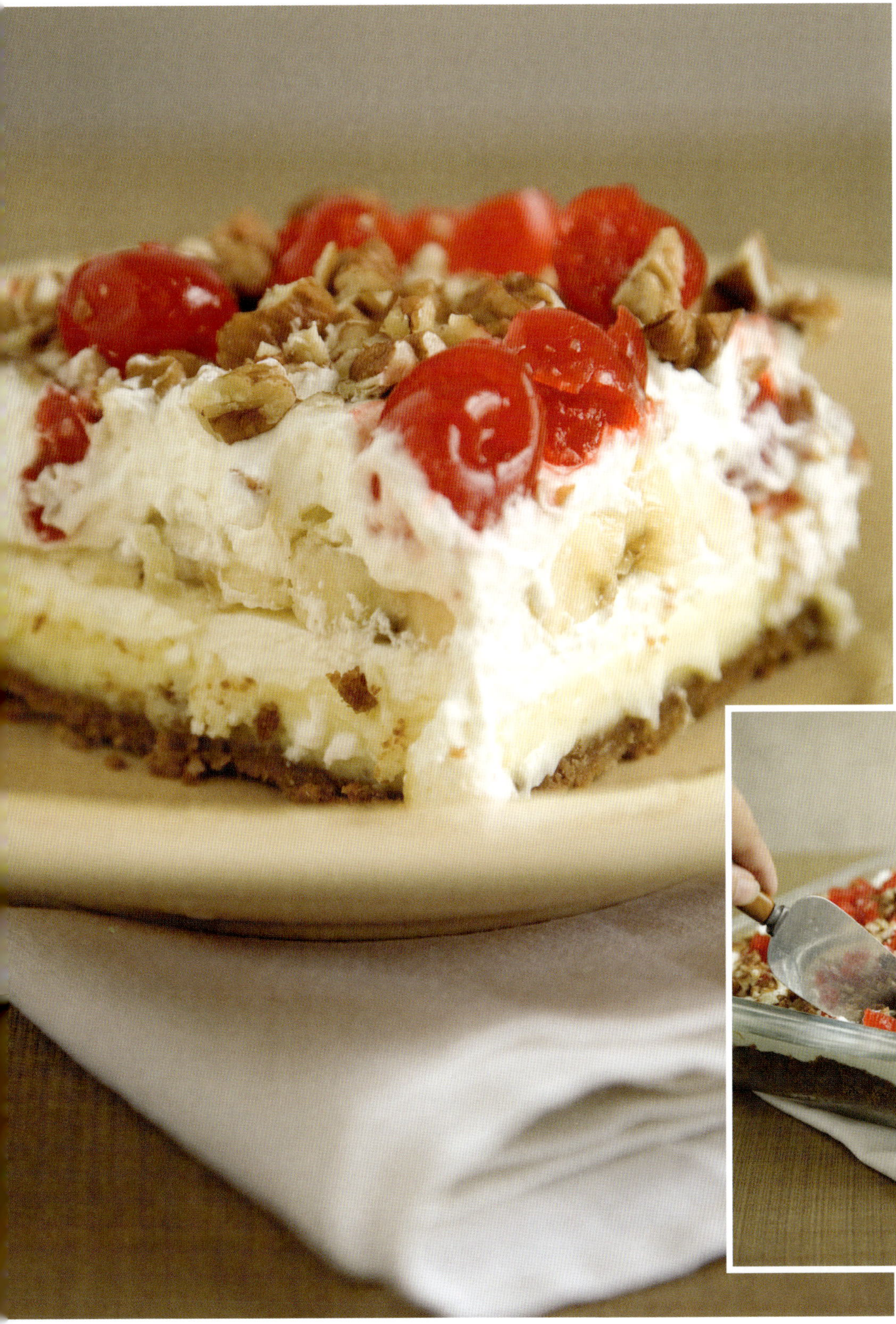
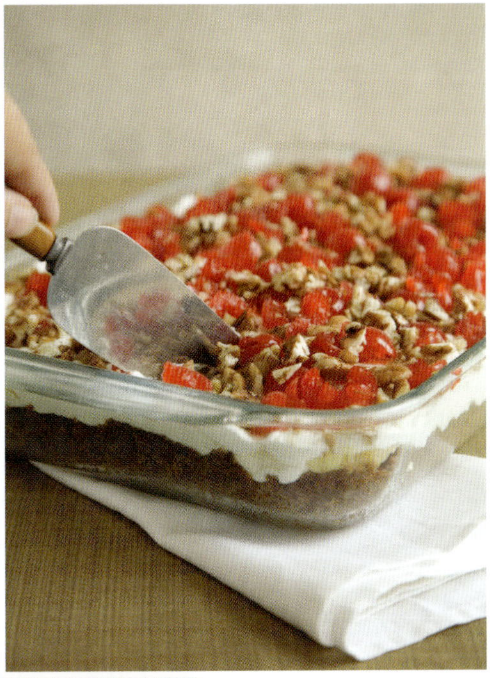

Butter Pecan Loaf

During the Christmas holidays, make several of these to give as gifts. This is also a great dessert to serve with homemade ice cream in the summer. Or, cut the cake into thick slices, toast and spread with jam, jelly, or preserves to enjoy for breakfast with a cup of café au lait.

Makes 8 to 10 servings

1 stick (8 tablespoons) unsalted butter

¼ cup pecan halves

2 cups all-purpose flour

1½ teaspoons baking powder

¼ teaspoon salt

4 eggs

1¼ cups sugar

⅔ cup heavy cream

6 tablespoons cognac

Preheat the oven to 325 degrees. Butter a 9x5x3-inch loaf pan. Line the bottom of the pan with waxed or parchment paper. Butter the paper, then dust the sides and bottom with flour. Shake off any excess. Set aside.

In a large skillet, melt the butter over medium-low heat. Add the pecans and cook, stirring, until the nuts are lightly toasted, 3 to 4 minutes.

Drain the nuts in a strainer placed over a measuring cup, tossing to remove as much butter as possible. There should be about ½ cup of melted butter in the cup. If there isn't, add enough melted butter to measure ½ cup. Let the butter cool to room temperature and set aside. Coarsely chop the pecans and set aside.

Sift together the flour, baking powder, and salt into a mixing bowl. In another mixing bowl, beat the eggs with an electric mixer on medium speed for about 30 seconds. Gradually add the sugar on medium-high speed and beat until the mixture is light and fluffy, about 5 minutes.

Add the cream and beat to blend. Reduce the speed to low, add the flour mixture, and beat until just blended. Scrape down the sides of the bowl; add the cognac and the chopped pecans. Stir to blend. Fold in the melted butter and pour the batter into the pan.

Bake until the cake is golden and the center springs back when touched, about 1½ hours. Cool the cake in the pan for about 10 minutes, then turn it over onto a wire rack to cool completely.

When it has cooled, wrap it in plastic wrap, then in foil. Let the cake stand for one day before slicing. It will keep up to one week.

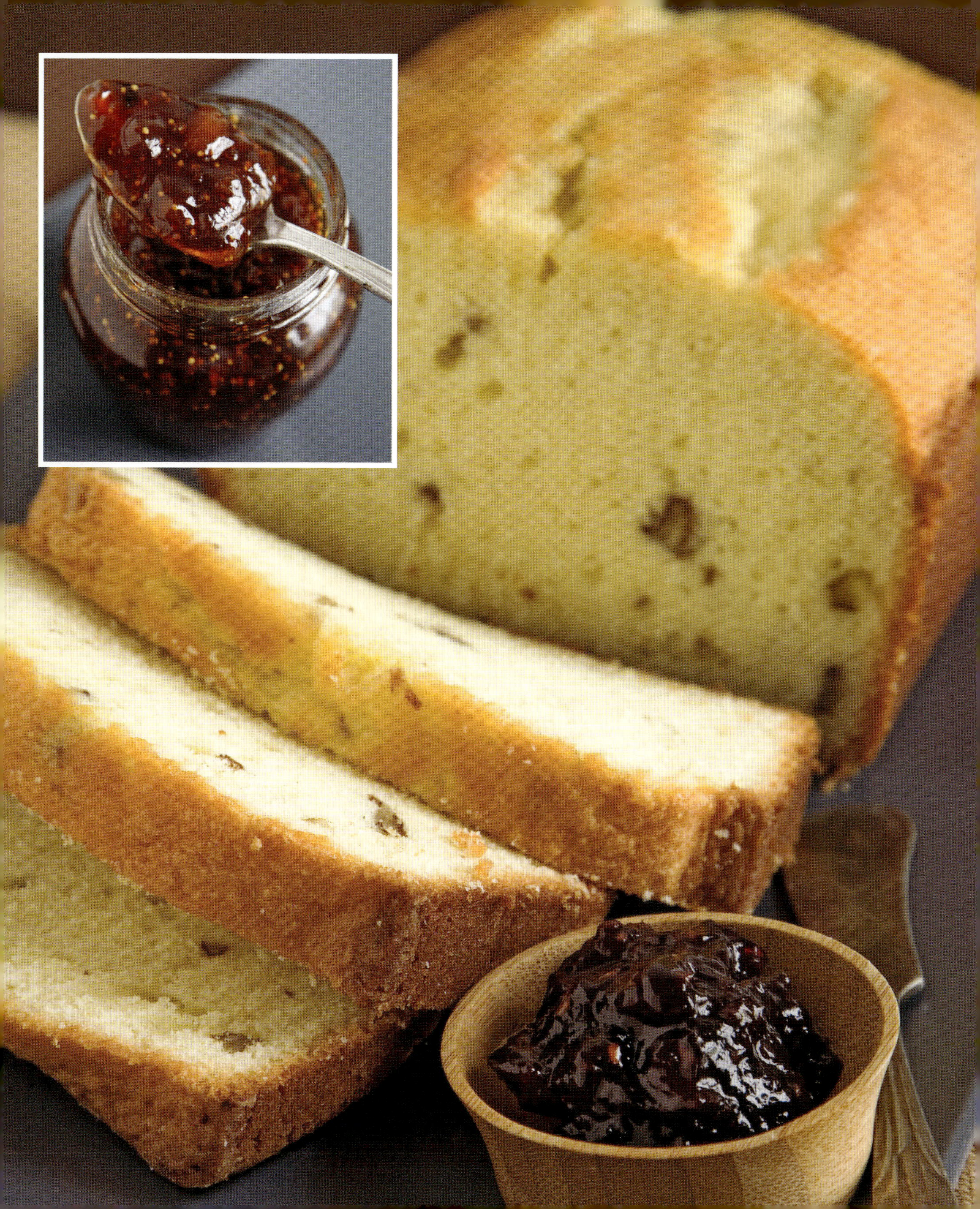

Overnight Coffee Cake

If you have weekend guests or want to treat your family to a fresh-from-the-oven breakfast, this is the way to go. The night before, prepare the coffee cake and store it in the refrigerator. Just pop it in the oven the next morning. Perhaps you had better make two batches—it's that good!

Makes 12 servings

2 cups all-purpose flour

1 cup sugar

1 cup firmly packed brown sugar

1 teaspoon baking soda

1 teaspoon baking powder

½ teaspoon salt

2 teaspoons ground cinnamon

1 cup buttermilk

10 tablespoons butter, melted

2 large eggs

½ cup chopped pecans

Butter and lightly flour a 9x13-inch baking pan.

Combine the flour, sugar, ½ cup of the brown sugar, baking soda, baking powder, salt, and 1 teaspoon of the cinnamon in a large mixing bowl. Mix well.

Add the buttermilk, butter, and eggs and beat at low speed with an electric mixer until moistened. Beat at medium speed for 3 minutes. Spoon the batter into the prepared pan.

Combine the remaining ½ cup brown sugar, the pecans, and the remaining 1 teaspoon of cinnamon and sprinkle over the batter. Cover and refrigerate for 8 to 12 hours.

Preheat the oven to 350 degrees. Uncover the cake and bake until lightly browned, 30 to 35 minutes. Serve warm.

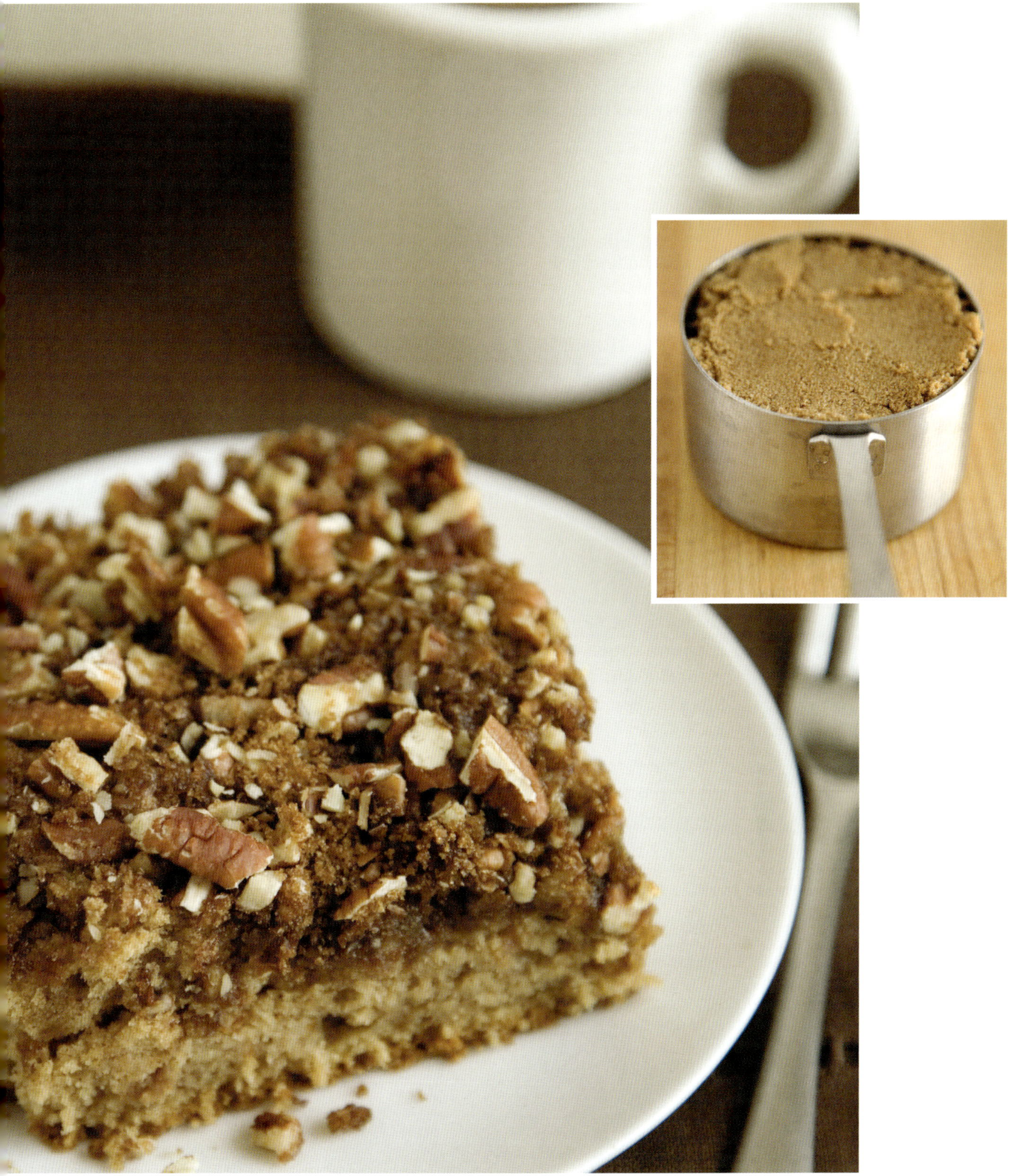

Pineapple Cake

Keith Courrégé called this a Cajun cake. Why? We don't really know, so we renamed it pineapple cake. However, we do know that this is a moist cake similar to a pineapple upside-down cake but baked in a large dish rather than in a skillet.

Makes 12 to 14 servings

Cake:

2 cups sugar

2 eggs

2 cups crushed pineapple with can syrup

1½ cups all-purpose flour

½ cup pecan meal

2½ teaspoons baking powder

¼ teaspoon salt

Icing:

½ stick (4 tablespoons) butter

½ cup packed light brown sugar

Pinch salt

¼ cup evaporated milk

2 cups confectioners' sugar

1 teaspoon pure vanilla extract

1 cup grated coconut

1 cup chopped pecans

To make the cake: Preheat the oven to 325 degrees. Grease and flour a 9x13-inch baking dish and set aside.

Cream the sugar and eggs with an electric mixer in a mixing bowl until light and fluffy. Add the pineapple, flour, pecan meal, baking powder, and salt. Mix to blend.

Pour the batter into the prepared pan and bake until a cake tester inserted in the center of the cake comes out clean, 30 to 35 minutes. Remove from the oven and cool completely.

In the meantime, prepare the icing.

To make the icing: Combine the butter, sugar, salt, and evaporated milk in the top of a double boiler over medium heat. Stir constantly until the mixture is smooth. Remove from the heat and cool for 15 minutes.

Beat in the confectioners' sugar until the mixture is of a spreading consistency. Stir in the vanilla, coconut, and pecans and mix well. Pour the icing over the cooled cake.

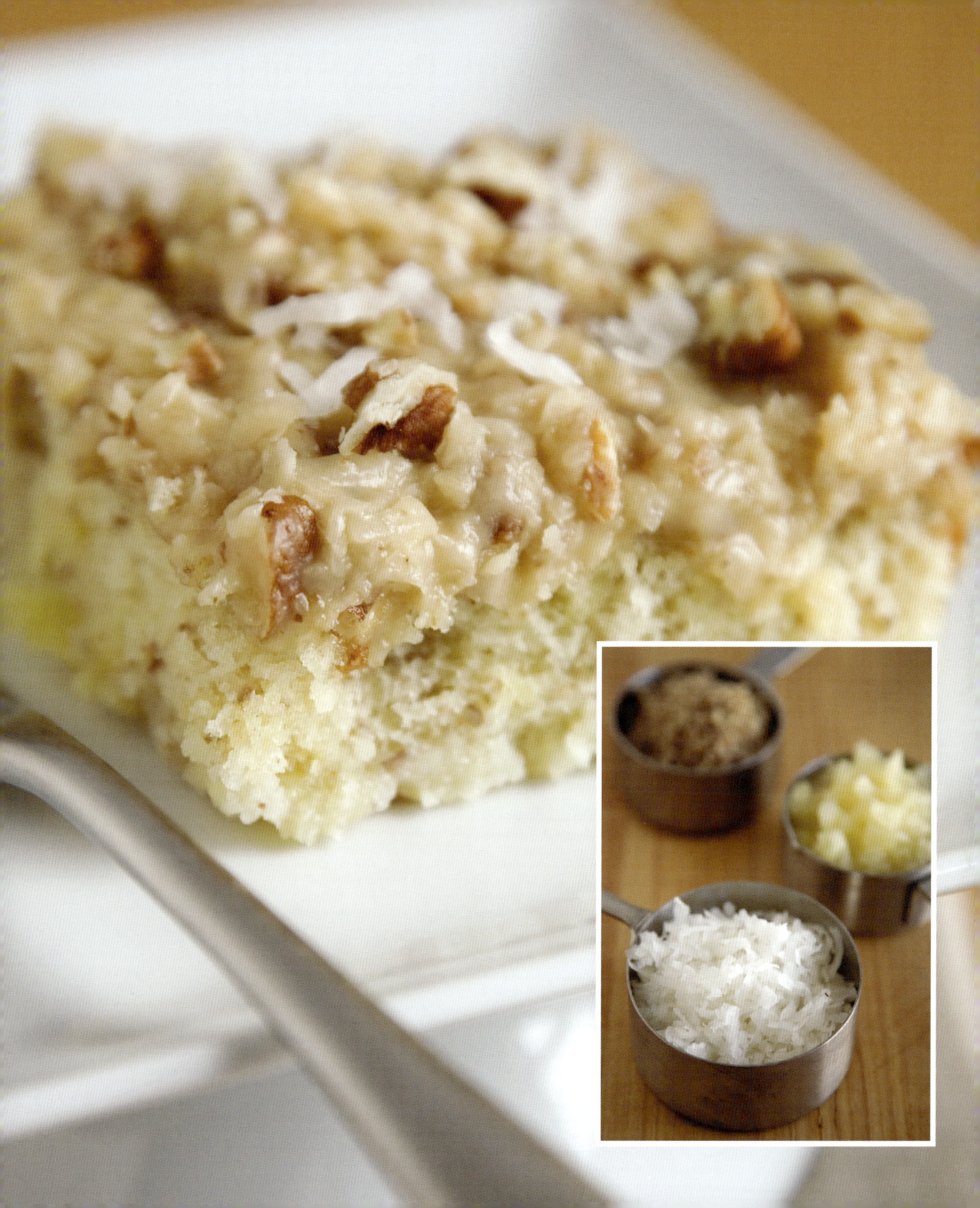

Fig Preserve Cake with Pecan Icing

Fig preserves are always terrific to spread on biscuits, cornbread, or toast, so if you have a penchant for those delectable preserves, you will love this cake. While it certainly can be served for dessert, it also can be served for breakfast for those who have an early-morning sweet tooth.

Makes 8 servings

Cake:

4 tablespoons butter, softened

3 tablespoons sugar

1 egg

1½ cups all-purpose flour

½ teaspoon baking soda

½ teaspoon salt

½ teaspoon baking powder

1 pint fig preserves, mashed

1 cup chopped pecans

1 teaspoon pure vanilla extract

Icing:

1 stick (8 tablespoons) butter, softened

1 cup pecan meal

2 cups confectioners' sugar

1 teaspoon pure vanilla extract

1 to 2 tablespoons milk

To make the cake: Preheat the oven to 350 degrees. Butter and flour a 9-inch square baking pan. Set aside.

Cream the butter and sugar in a mixing bowl with an electric mixer until light and fluffy. Add the egg and beat well by hand.

Sift the flour, baking soda, salt, and baking powder into another mixing bowl. Add the figs, pecans, and vanilla and stir to mix. Add the butter-sugar mixture and mix well.

Spread the batter into the prepared pan and bake until a cake tester inserted in the center comes out clean, 30 to 40 minutes. Remove the cake from the oven and cool in the pan for several minutes before turning onto a wire rack to cool completely.

Meanwhile, prepare the icing.

To make the icing: Combine the butter, pecan meal, confectioners' sugar, and vanilla in a mixing bowl and stir to blend. Add enough milk to make a spreading consistency.

Spread the icing on the top and sides of the cooled cake.

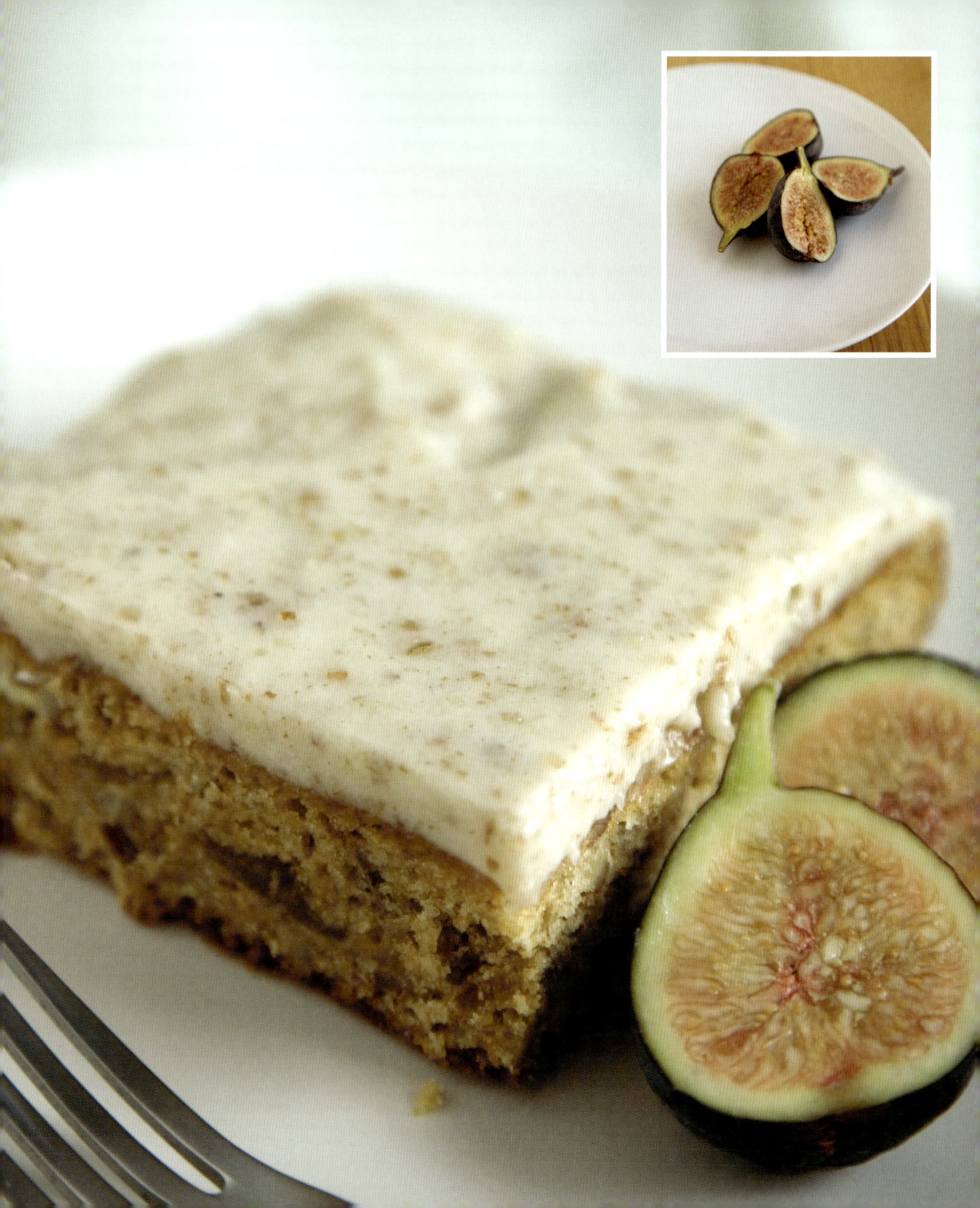

The Best-Ever Brownies

Brownies are a favorite chocolate treat, and these are indeed the best ever! Carry them along on a picnic or have them ready for an after-school treat for children, but be aware that adults will also love these rich brownies.

Makes about 1 dozen

Brownie:

4 1-ounce squares unsweetened chocolate

2 sticks (½ pound) butter

1 cup granulated sugar

1 cup packed light brown sugar

4 eggs

½ cup all-purpose flour

½ cup pecan meal

1 teaspoon pure vanilla extract

¼ teaspoon salt

2 cups coarsely chopped pecans

Icing:

1 stick (8 tablespoons) butter

¼ cup unsweetened cocoa powder

2 tablespoons honey

3 tablespoons heavy cream

1 pound confectioners' sugar, sifted

To make the brownie: Preheat the oven to 325 degrees. Lightly butter a 9-inch square baking pan and set aside.

Melt the chocolate and butter in a heavy saucepan over very low heat. Gradually beat in the granulated and brown sugars and stir until they are completely dissolved.

Add the eggs, one at a time, incorporating each one before adding another. Add the flour, pecan meal, vanilla extract, salt, and the chopped pecans. Stir to mix well.

Pour the batter into the prepared pan and bake until a cake tester inserted in the center comes out clean, 30 to 35 minutes. Remove from the oven and cool.

Meanwhile, prepare the icing.

To make the icing: Combine all the ingredients in a bowl and whisk until smooth. If the mixture is too thin, add more sugar, if too thick, add more cream. Spread the icing over the cooled brownie and cut into squares.

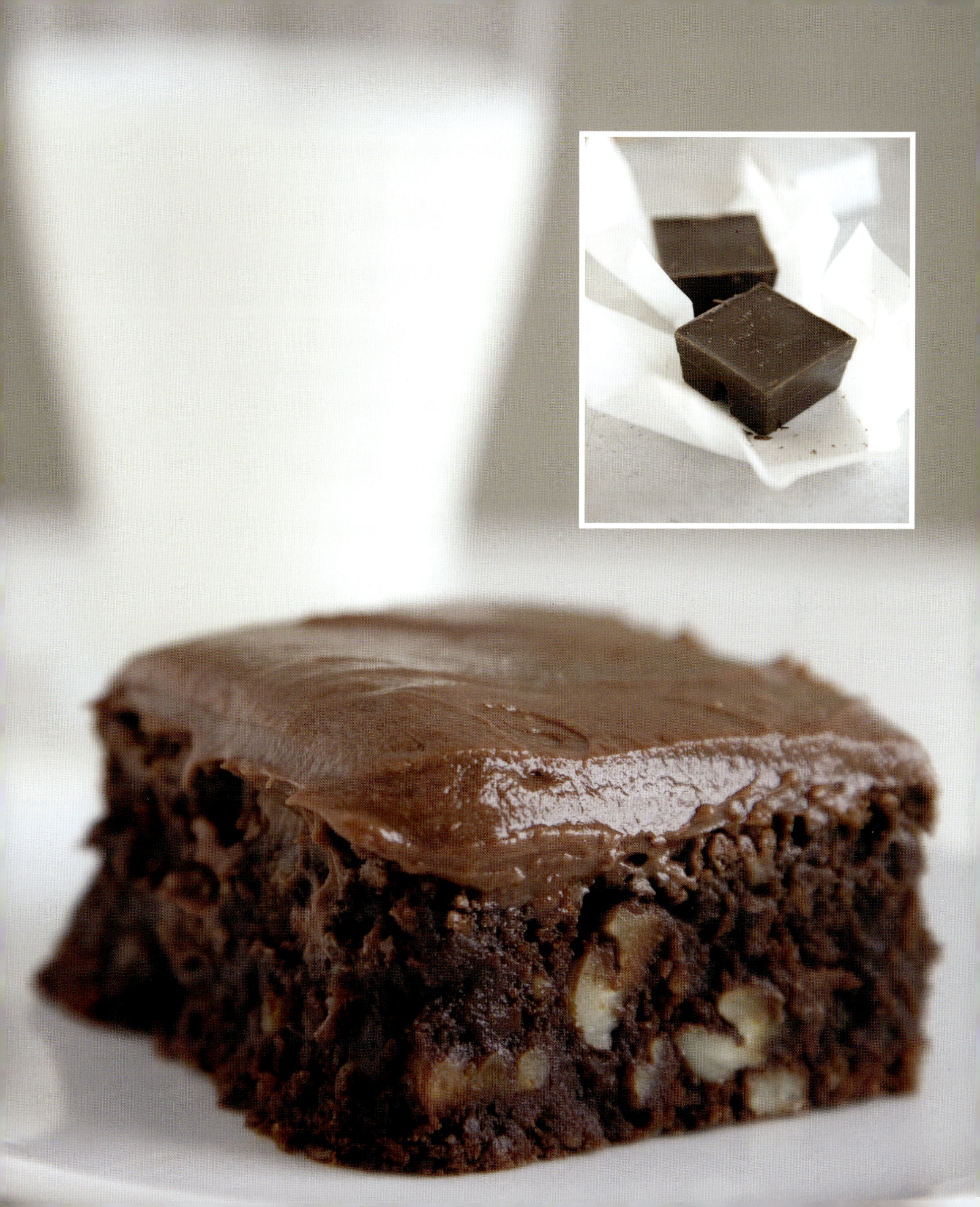

Chocolate Orange Pecan Torte

The cake layers are made with butter, sugar, eggs, pecan meal, and a little flour. The result is a thin rich cake layered with an orange-flavored chocolate mixture and iced with buttercream. Because of the richness of the dessert, a small wedge is more than enough for each serving. Once the cake is assembled, chill it for at least two hours.

Makes 8 to 10 servings

Cake:

2 sticks (½ pound) butter, softened

1 cup sugar

4 eggs

1½ cups pecan meal

½ cup all-purpose flour

⅓ cup milk

2 tablespoons orange-flavored liqueur

1 tablespoon grated orange zest

¼ teaspoon salt

To make the cake: Preheat the oven to 300 degrees. Butter and lightly flour two 9-inch cake pans. Set aside.

Cream the butter and sugar with an electric mixer in a mixing bowl until light and fluffy. Add the eggs, one at a time, beating well after each addition. Stir in the pecan meal, then add the flour alternately with the milk. Add the liqueur, orange zest, and salt. Stir to blend.

Divide the batter evenly between the prepared cake pans and bake until just firm to the touch, about 1 hour.

Remove the cakes from the oven and cool for a few minutes. Gently run a thin, small knife around the sides of the pan to loosen, then carefully transfer cake to a wire rack to cool completely.

Meanwhile, prepare the icing and the filling.

To make the icing: Cream the butter and sugar with an electric mixer in a mixing bowl until light and fluffy. Blend in the remaining ingredients. Divide the mixture in half. Set aside.

To make the filling: Melt the chocolate in the top of a double boiler over hot, but not boiling water. Remove from the heat and cool slightly. Add the chocolate to half of the icing mixture and mix well to blend. Spread the filling between the two layers of cake, and frost the top and sides with the remaining icing.

Decorate the top of the cake with pecan halves and chocolate sprinkles or orange slices.

Chill well before serving.

Icing:
2 sticks (½ pound) butter, softened

1 pound confectioners' sugar

2 tablespoons fresh orange juice

1 tablespoon grated orange zest

1 tablespoon orange-flavored liqueur

Pecan halves and chocolate sprinkles or orange slices for garnish

Filling:
4 1-ounce squares semisweet chocolate

½ recipe Orange Icing

Macaroon Pie

If you like coconut and pecans, then the combination is a winner in this crunchy pie. Let the pie cool down a bit after baking before cutting into wedges.

Makes 6 servings

1 9-inch unbaked pie shell

3 eggs, lightly beaten

1 cup light corn syrup

½ cup packed light brown sugar

3 tablespoons butter, melted

½ teaspoon pure almond extract

Pinch of salt

1 cup grated coconut

1 cup coarsely chopped pecans

Whipped cream for serving

Preheat the oven to 350 degrees. Place the pie shell in a 9-inch deep-dish pie pan and set aside.

Combine the eggs with the corn syrup, brown sugar, butter, almond extract, and salt in a large mixing bowl and beat, by hand, until well mixed.

Fold in the coconut and pecans and pour into the pie crust. Bake until the center sets, 40 to 50 minutes. Remove from the oven and cool.

Serve topped with whipped cream.

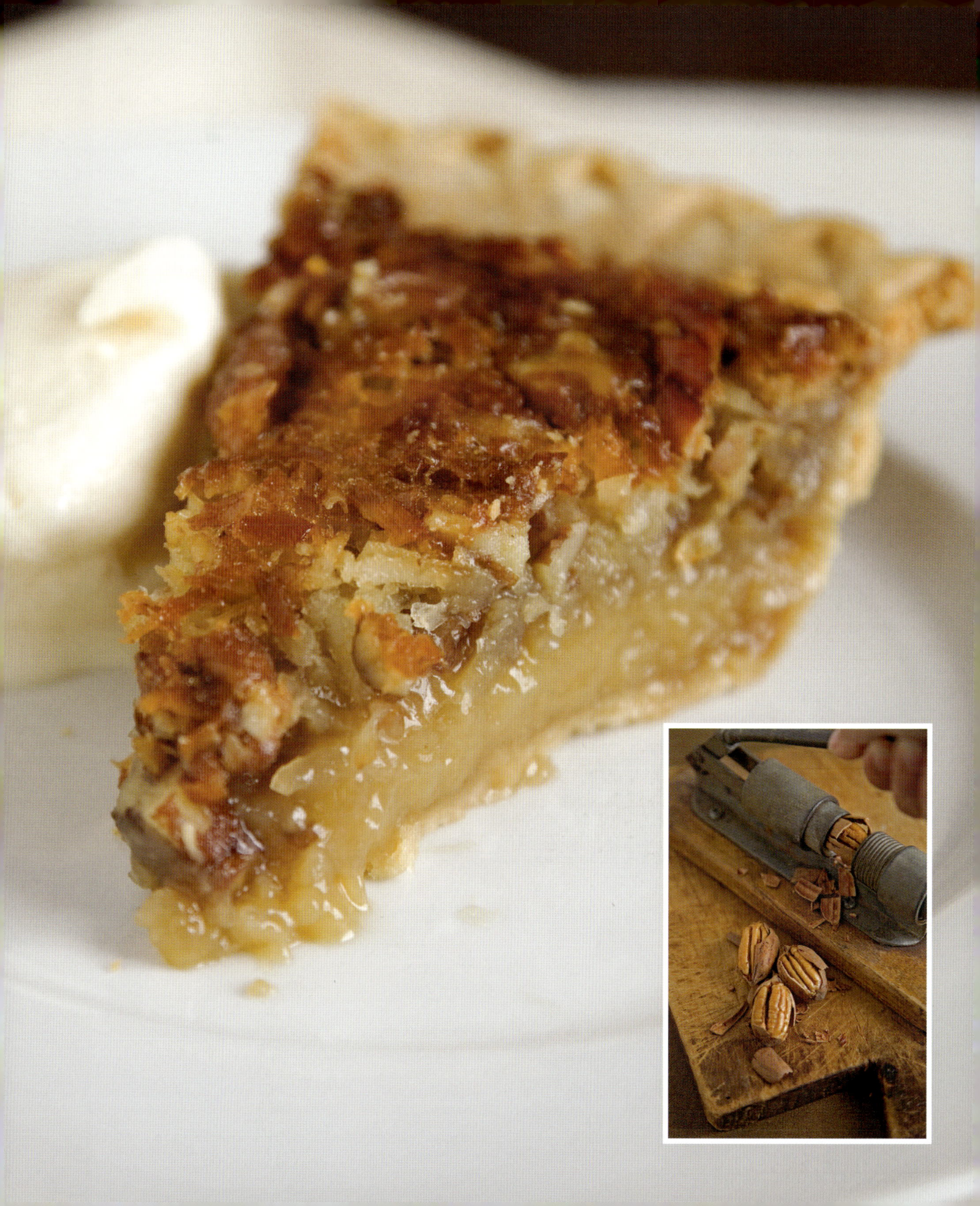

Olivia's Perfect Pecan Pie

Jady Regard believes this pecan pie recipe from his wife, Olivia, is the best—hands down! It is the molasses, he says, that gives it a superb flavor. We think you will agree.

Makes 6 to 8 servings

3 eggs

1 cup sugar

¾ cup light corn syrup

¼ cup Steen's Molasses

⅛ teaspoon salt

2 teaspoons vanilla extract

½ cup melted butter, slightly cooled

1 refrigerated pie-crust dough

1 cup of pecan halves, toasted and coarsely chopped

Preheat the oven to 350 degrees.

Beat the eggs in a mixing bowl. Add the sugar, corn syrup, molasses, salt, vanilla, and butter. Stir to blend.

According to the package directions, place the pie-crust dough in a pie pan and crimp the edges. Arrange the pecans in a single layer on the bottom of the pie crust. Pour the filling over the pecans and bake for 1 hour.

Allow pie to cool before serving.

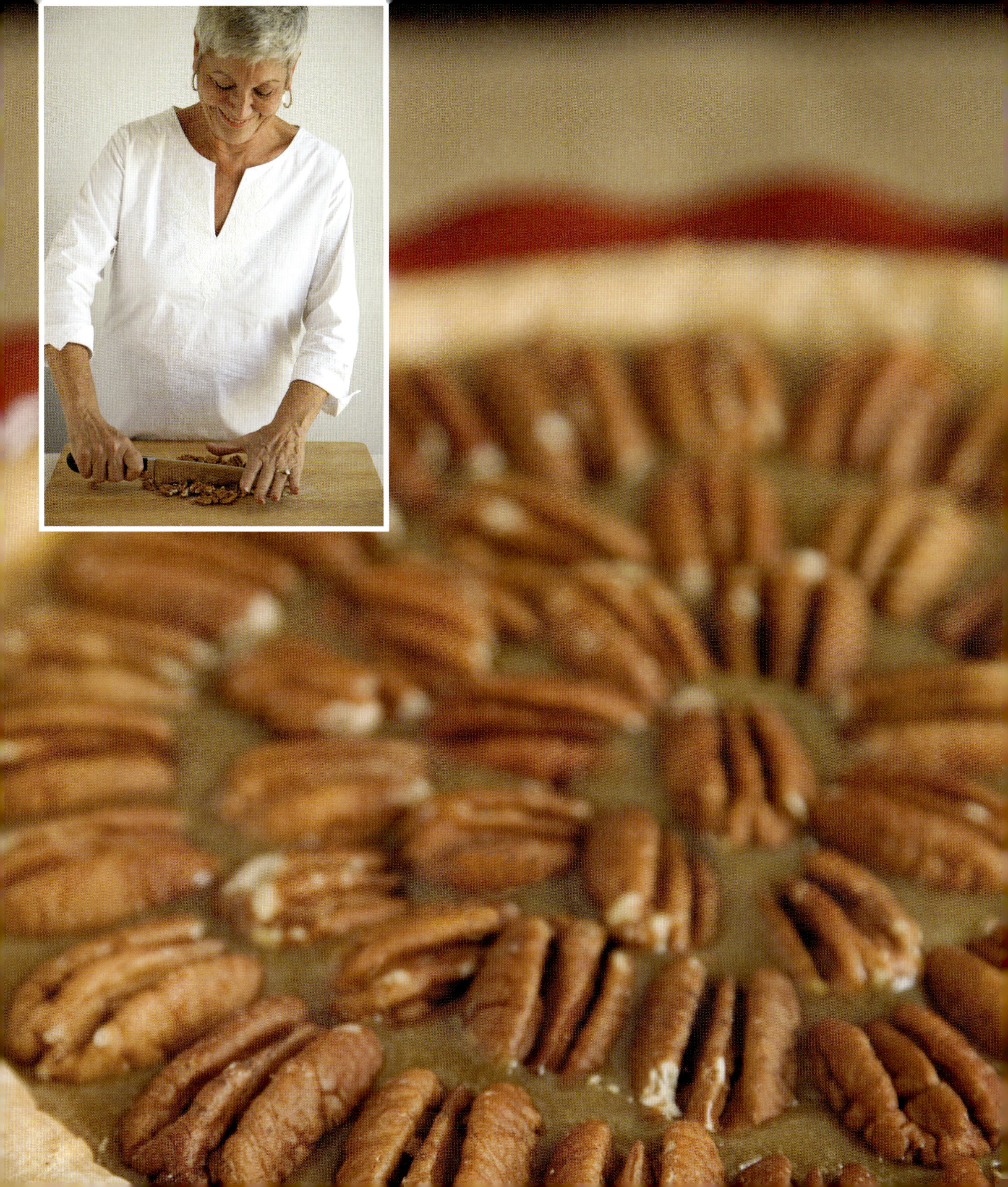

Butterscotch Pecan Pie

This is a different and delightful twist on the classic pecan pie. The butterscotch flavor just begs for a scoop of ice cream or a dollop of whipped cream—marvelous!

Makes 6 servings

1 stick (8 tablespoons) butter

¾ cup packed dark brown sugar

¼ cup water

2 tablespoons dark corn syrup

4 tablespoons cornstarch

½ cup granulated sugar

¼ teaspoon salt

¼ cup milk

¼ cup evaporated milk

2 egg yolks, lightly beaten

1 9-inch prebaked pie shell

1 cup coarsely chopped toasted pecans

Sweetened Whipped Cream (recipe follows)

Combine the butter, brown sugar, water, and corn syrup in a heavy saucepan over medium heat and stir until the mixture reaches the soft-ball stage (235 degrees on a candy thermometer).

Remove from the heat and set aside.

Combine the cornstarch, granulated sugar, and salt in another heavy saucepan over medium heat. Add the milks and beaten eggs and cook, stirring constantly, until the mixture is thick and smooth. Remove from the heat and add the brown sugar mixture. Stir until completely blended.

Pour the mixture into the pie shell and sprinkle with the pecans. Cool completely, then refrigerate until the filling sets, 2 to 3 hours.

Serve with the Sweetened Whipped Cream.

Sweetened Whipped Cream

Combine the cream, vanilla, and sugar in a mixing bowl and whip with an electric mixer until soft peaks form.

Makes about 2 cups

1½ cups heavy cream

1 teaspoon pure vanilla extract

3 teaspoons sugar

Pecan Tartlets

These small pecan tartlets don't last long, so make several batches to store in the freezer. Serve them with ice cream for a dinner party dessert, offer them at cocktail parties, or keep them on hand to enjoy with a cup of coffee anytime. By all means, give them as gifts to anyone who likes a rich, sweet treat.

Makes 48

Pastry:
1 8-ounce package cream cheese, softened

2 sticks margarine

2 cups all-purpose flour

Filling:
3 eggs, well beaten

2 cups brown sugar

4 cups chopped pecans

1 teaspoon vanilla extract

To make the pastry: Combine the cream cheese, margarine, and flour and blend together. Separate into 6 equal portions, then divide each portion into 8. Press the dough into tart tins or small muffin tins.

To make the filling: Combine the eggs, brown sugar, pecans, and vanilla. Pour into the lined tart tins; fill only ¾ full. Bake at 350 degrees for 20 minutes.

Cool a bit before removing them from the tins. After they are baked and cooled, they can be frozen in an airtight container.

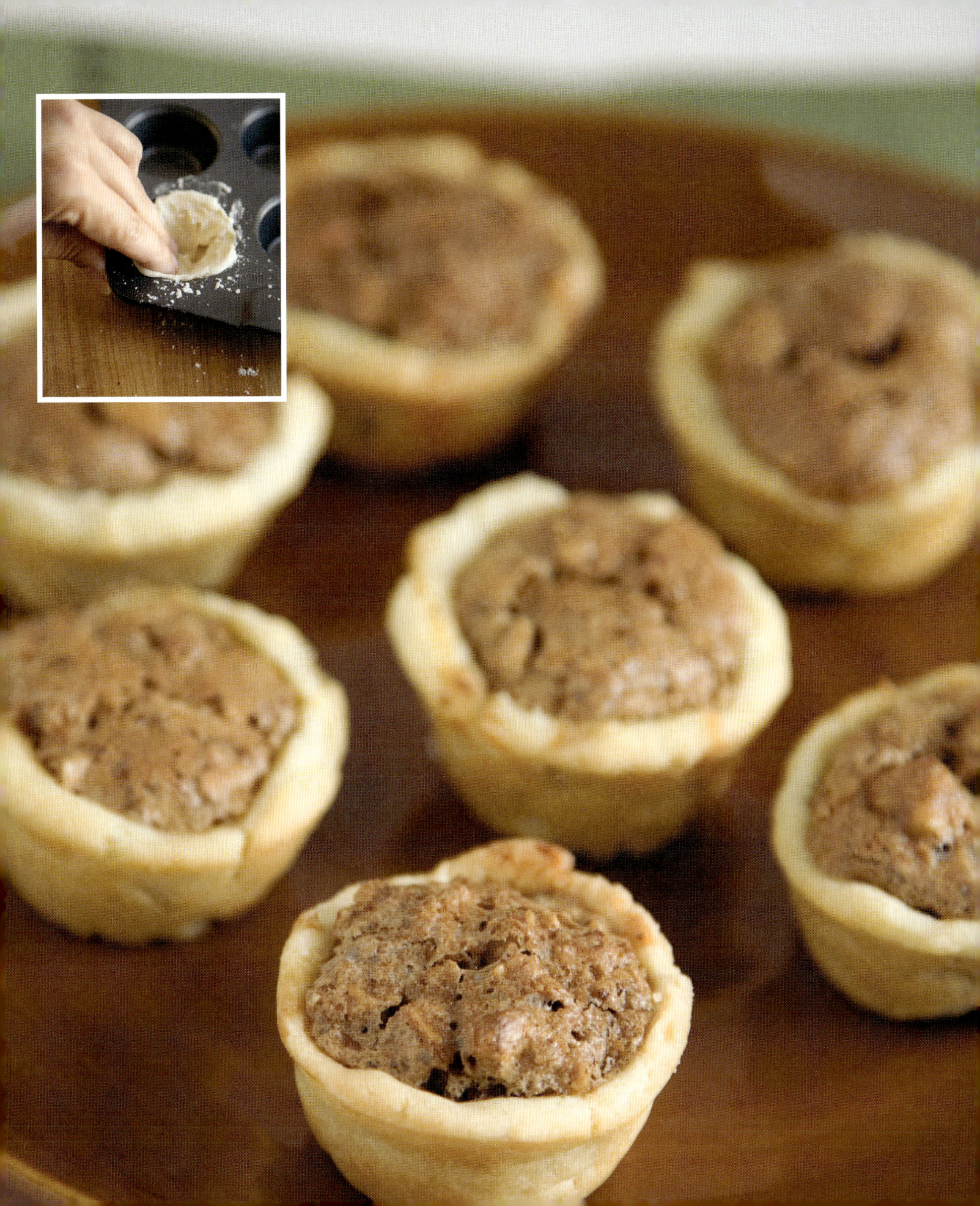

Les Oreilles de Cochon

These "pigs' ears" are a delightful Cajun treat to make for Halloween as well as for other holiday events. Children love these pastries!

Be sure to use pure cane syrup; no other syrup will do.

Makes 4 to 5 dozen

1 egg

½ cup milk

2 cups all-purpose flour

2 teaspoons baking powder

½ teaspoon salt

Vegetable oil for deep-frying

1 cup pure cane syrup

1 cup chopped pecans

Beat the egg until foamy. Add the milk and blend.

In a separate bowl, sift the flour, baking powder, and salt together twice. Add to the egg mixture and blend.

Cut off a small portion of the dough, about the size of a large pecan, and roll out on a lightly floured board until very thin.

Fill a deep, heavy pot with about 3 inches of vegetable oil and heat to 350 degrees.

Drop 1 piece of the dough at a time into the hot oil. With a long-handled fork, pierce the dough in the center and give it a good twist, holding it with the fork until it holds the form of a "pig's ear." Fry until light brown and drain on paper towels.

In a saucepan, boil the syrup until it reaches the soft-ball state (235 degrees on a candy thermometer) and drizzle over the fried pastries. While the syrup is still warm, scatter the chopped pecans over the pastries.

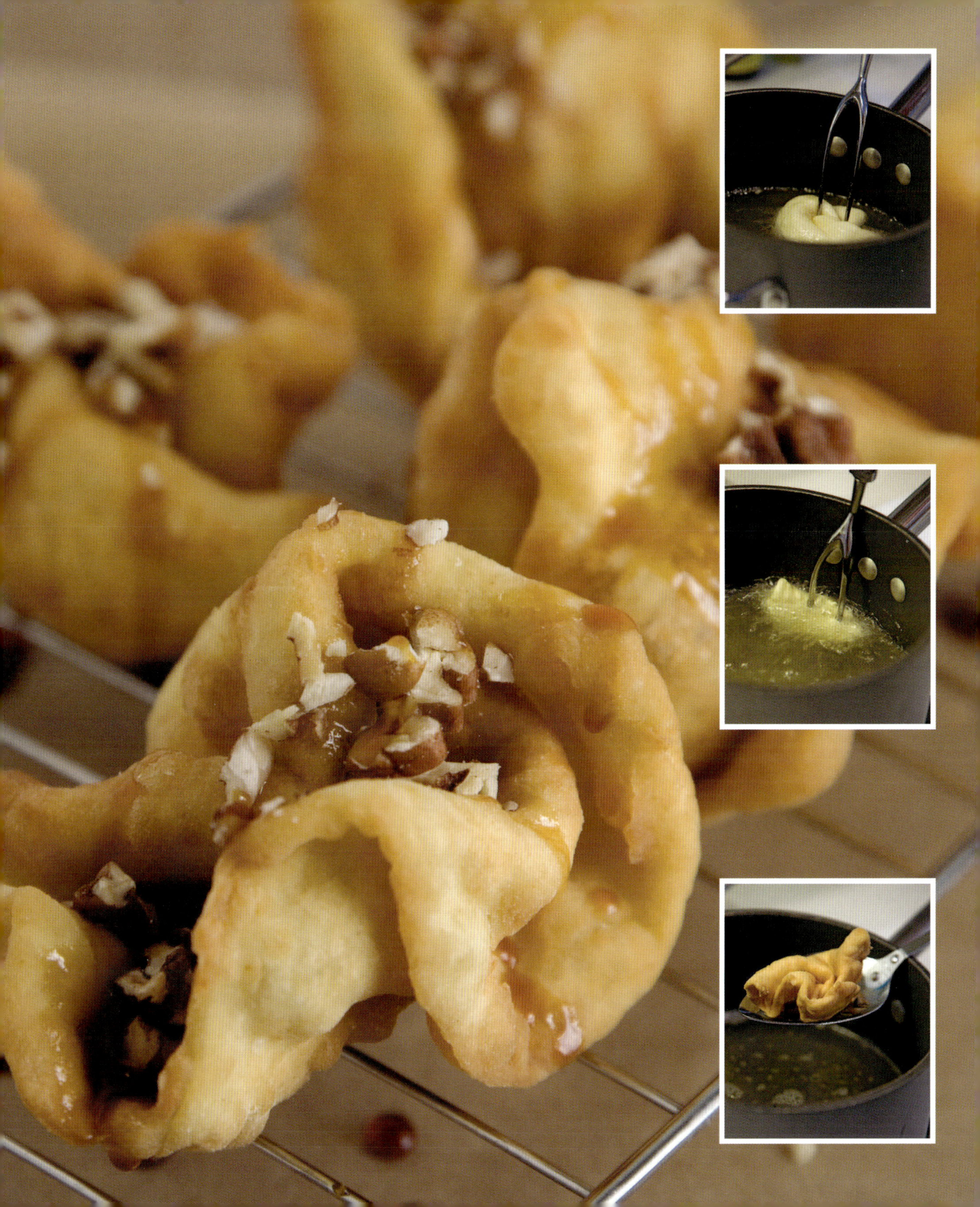

Rum-Bourbon Balls

Another holiday favorite, these rum-bourbon balls can be made ahead of time and stored between wax paper in an airtight container for several days. Bet you can't eat just one!

Makes 3 dozen

3 cups vanilla wafer crumbs

1 cup confectioners' sugar plus more for coating

1½ tablespoons unsweetened cocoa powder

3 tablespoons light corn syrup

⅓ cup dark rum

3 tablespoons bourbon or brandy

1 cup pecan meal

Combine all the ingredients in a mixing bowl and mix well. Form the mixture into balls the size of pecans and roll gently in confectioners' sugar.

Store in an airtight container for up to 1 week.

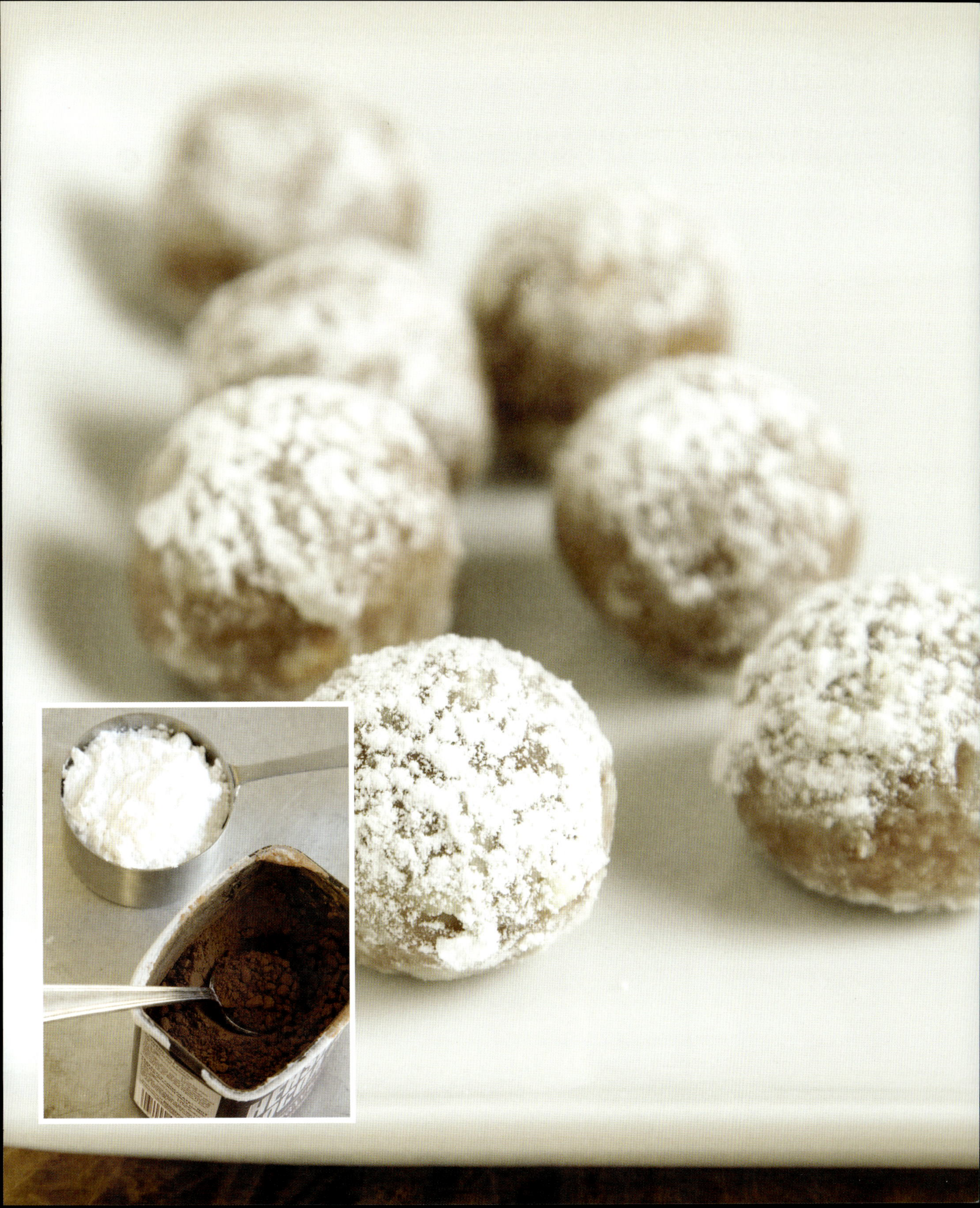

Pecan Pralines

Around the Christmas holidays, pralines are made by the dozen all over the South, but they can certainly be enjoyed year-round. Crumble the pralines and sprinkle on ice cream for an over-the-top dessert.

It's best to make the creamy confections on a clear, cold day or else they won't set up as well. Always use a candy thermometer when making pralines and other candies.

Makes about 2 dozen

2 cups packed light brown sugar

1 cup granulated sugar

1 cup evaporated milk

3 tablespoons light corn syrup

4 tablespoons butter

Pinch of salt

2½ to 3 cups pecan halves (depending on the size)

2 teaspoons pure vanilla extract

Combine the brown sugar, granulated sugar, evaporated milk, corn syrup, butter, and salt in a heavy saucepan over medium heat. Cook, stirring, until the sugar dissolves completely and the mixture begins to thicken.

Add the pecans and cook to the soft-ball stage (235 degrees on a candy thermometer). Add the vanilla and beat vigorously for a few minutes until the mixture begins to lose its gloss and becomes creamy.

Working quickly, drop by spoonfuls onto wax paper. If the candy becomes too hard, add 1 tablespoon of boiling water, place over very low heat and beat until it smoothes out.

Variation: Substitute 1 14-ounce can condensed milk for the 1 cup evaporated milk and proceed according to the recipe.

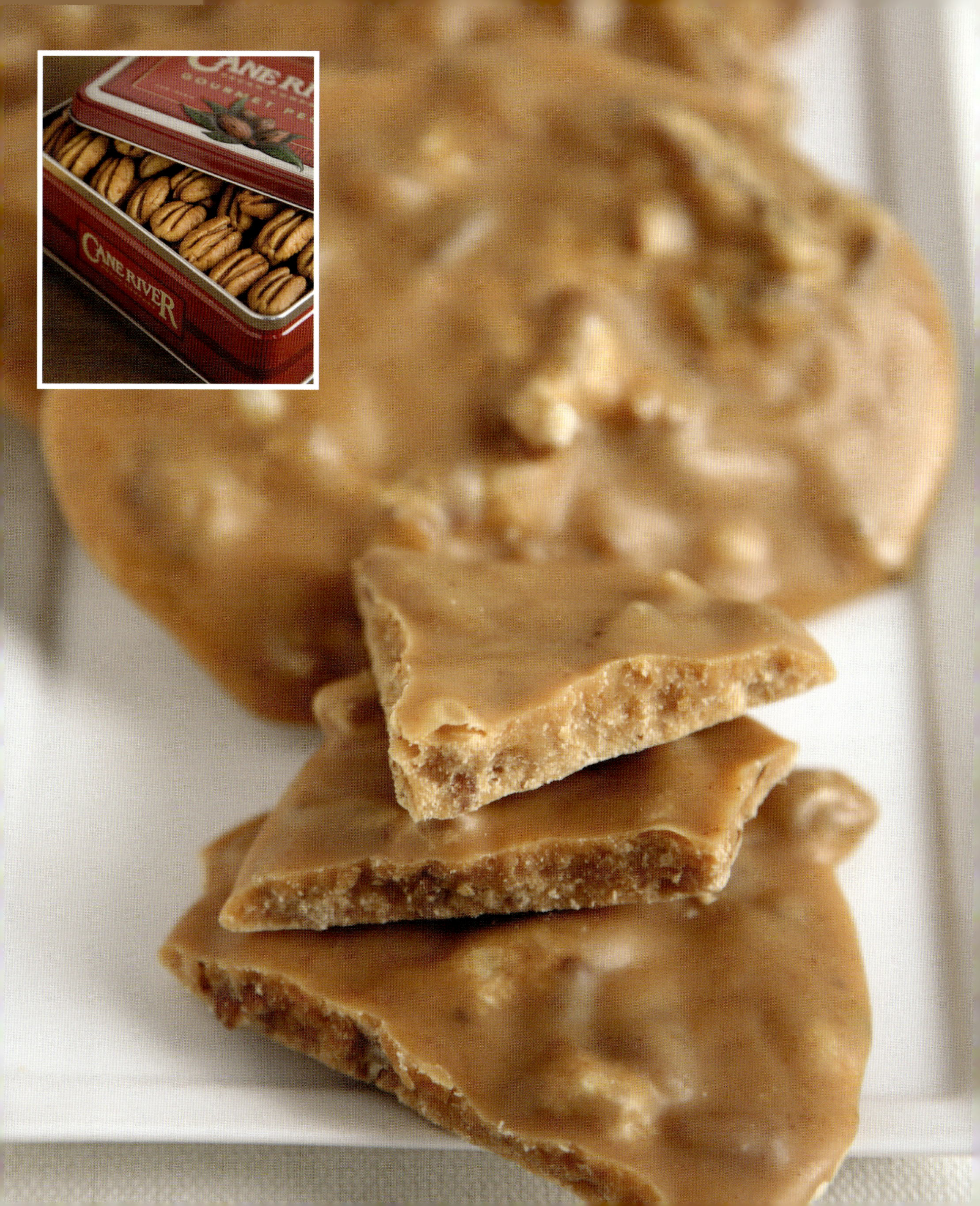
CANE RIVER

Buttermilk Fudge

This buttermilk fudge recipe is easy to make and palate pleasing. You should prepare several batches of this fudge to store in airtight containers to have on hand during the holidays when guests drop in unexpectedly or to have for gift-giving.

Note: It is always best to make fudge and pralines on a clear, cool day or else the candy will not set up properly. If you must, turn your air-conditioner on to be sure your kitchen is cool.

Makes about 1½ dozen

2½ cups sugar

1¼ cups buttermilk

4 tablespoons butter

1 teaspoon baking soda

2 tablespoons light corn syrup

1 teaspoon pure vanilla extract

2 cups chopped pecans

Butter a 7x11-inch baking dish.

Combine the sugar, buttermilk, butter, baking soda, and syrup in a heavy saucepan over medium heat. Stir constantly until the mixture reaches the soft-ball stage (235 degrees on a candy thermometer).

Remove from the heat; stir in the vanilla and pecans. Beat slightly and pour into the prepared pan. Cool and cut into squares.

Store in an airtight container.

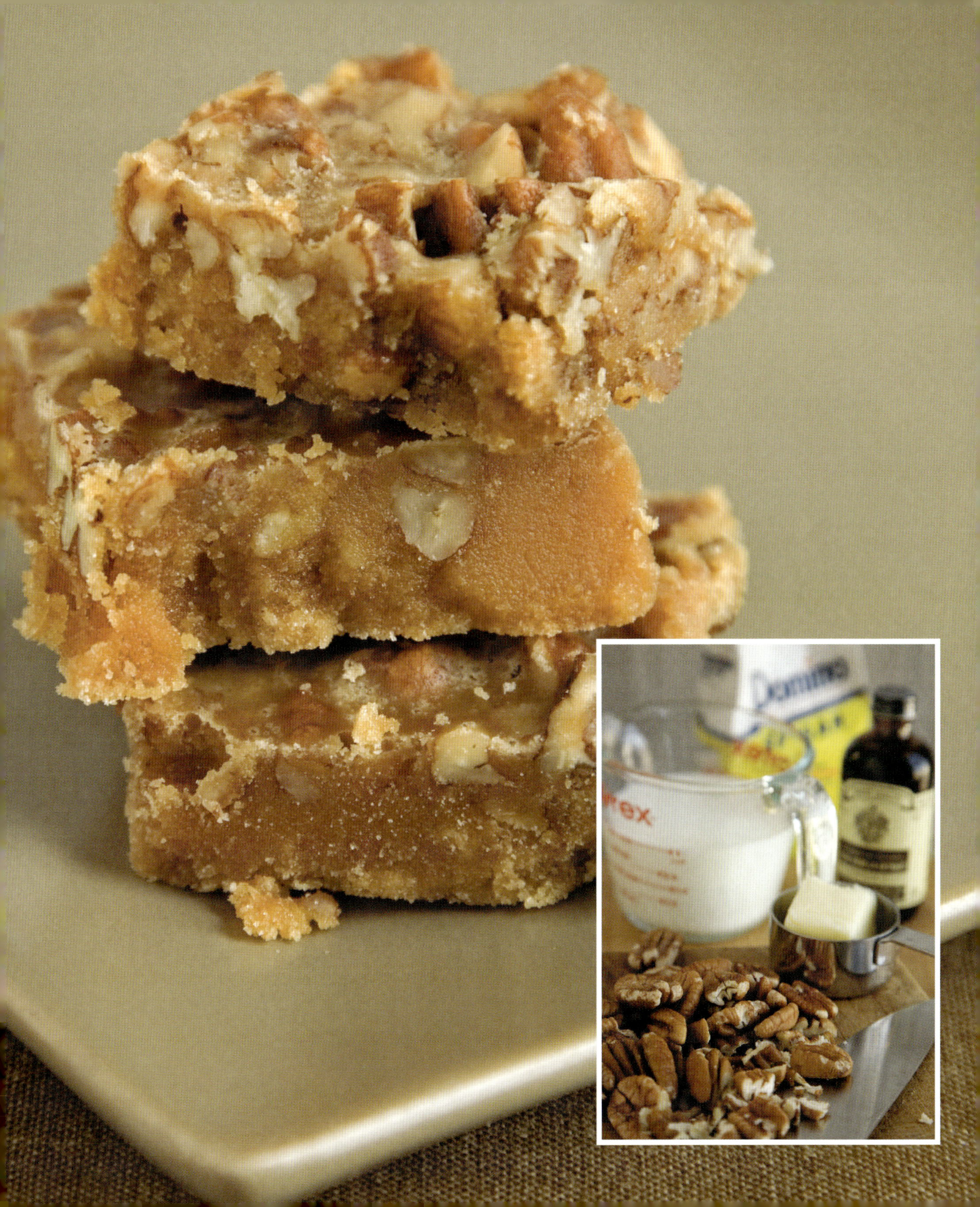

Butter Pecan Turtles

A crunchy crust coupled with the pecans and melted chocolate make these cookielike candy bars a go-to staple for lunch boxes. Alternatively, offer them as an after-dinner sweet or serve at a casual get-together. If you like, you can add another layer of chopped pecans over the melted chocolate—decadent!

Once they have cooled and been cut into squares, store them in an airtight container in a cool, dry place or in the refrigerator.

Makes about 48 squares

2 cups all-purpose flour

1½ cups packed dark brown sugar

½ cup plus ⅔ cup butter, softened

1¼ cups chopped pecans

12 ounces semisweet chocolate chips

Preheat the oven to 350 degrees.

Combine the flour, 1 cup of the brown sugar, and ½ cup of the butter in a mixing bowl and blend well. Press the mixture into an ungreased 9x13-inch baking dish. Sprinkle the top of the crust evenly with pecans.

Combine the remaining ⅔ cup butter and ½ cup brown sugar in a saucepan over medium heat and cook, stirring constantly, for 1 minute. Pour the mixture evenly over the pecans.

Bake until bubbly, about 20 minutes. Remove from the oven and immediately sprinkle the chocolate chips over the top and allow them to melt. Spread evenly to cover the surface. Cool and cut into squares.

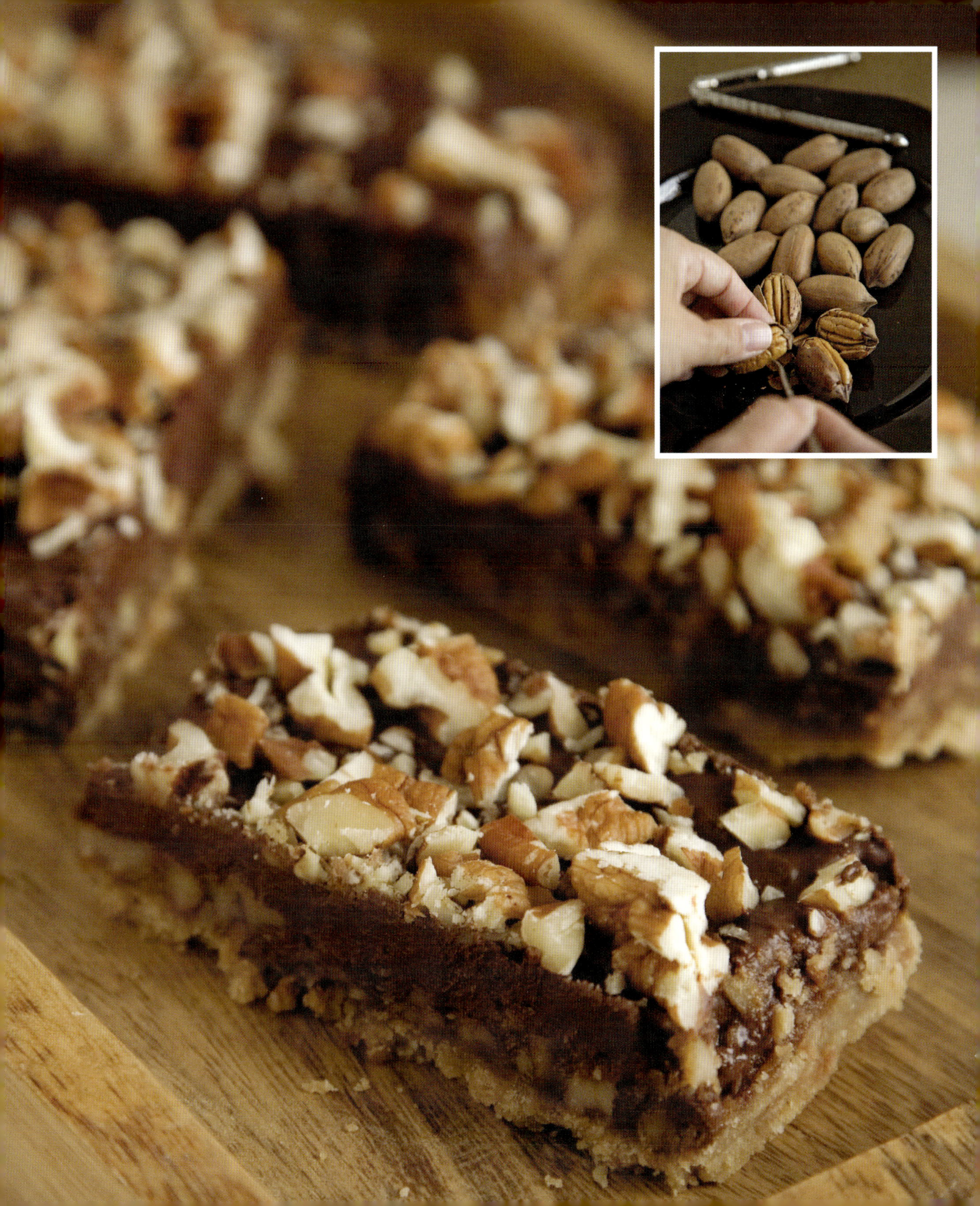

Pecan Truffles

Truffles are sinfully delicious. After a rich meal, offer these for dessert to serve with coffee, or better yet, try them with a glass of good port wine. Of course, they make delightful gifts for chocolate lovers—put them in small candy cups and pack them in decorative airtight containers.

Makes about 2½ dozen

6 1-ounce squares semisweet chocolate

⅓ cup heavy cream

¾ cup pecan meal

1⅓ cups confectioners' sugar

1 tablespoon orange liqueur, such as Grand Marnier or Cointreau

⅓ cup unsweetened cocoa, sifted

Combine the chocolate and cream in a heavy saucepan over low heat. Cook, stirring, until the chocolate is completely melted. Add the pecan meal, sugar, and liqueur. Stir to blend.

Remove from the heat and pour into a bowl. Cover loosely with plastic wrap and refrigerate until completely cooled and firm.

Put the cocoa in a shallow bowl. Using a small melon baller or small scoop, scoop out the chocolate mixture and quickly roll into a ball in the palms of your hands.

Drop into the cocoa and roll to coat evenly.

Store between wax paper in an airtight container in the refrigerator for up to 2 weeks.

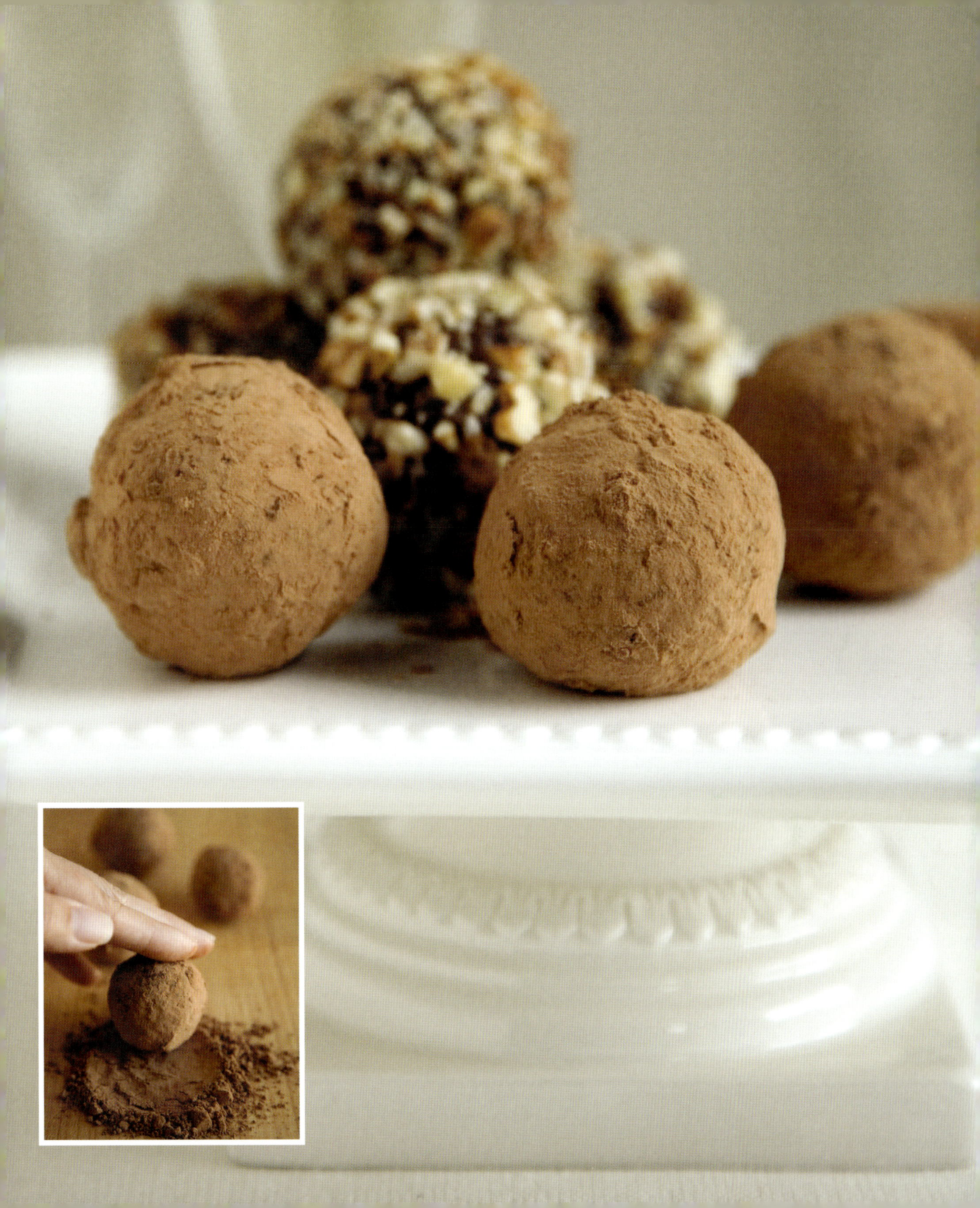

Pecan Martini

And last, but not least, a bit of lagniappe (something extra) to further please your palate—our pecan martini. Pecan liqueur is available at most fine liquor stores. (See Source Guide for more information.)

It is best to chill both the vodka and liqueur to enhance the flavor of the drink. Make this drink your very own by experimenting with flavored vodkas.

Makes 1 drink

1 martini glass, chilled

1½ ounces pecan liqueur, chilled

2 teaspoons pecan meal

2 ounces vodka, chilled

1 lightly toasted pecan half

Put ½ ounce of the pecan liqueur into a coffee cup saucer. Add the pecan meal to another saucer. Dip the rim of a martini glass first in the pecan liqueur, then in the pecan meal.

Add the remaining pecan liqueur and the vodka to the glass and drop in the pecan half. Serve immediately.

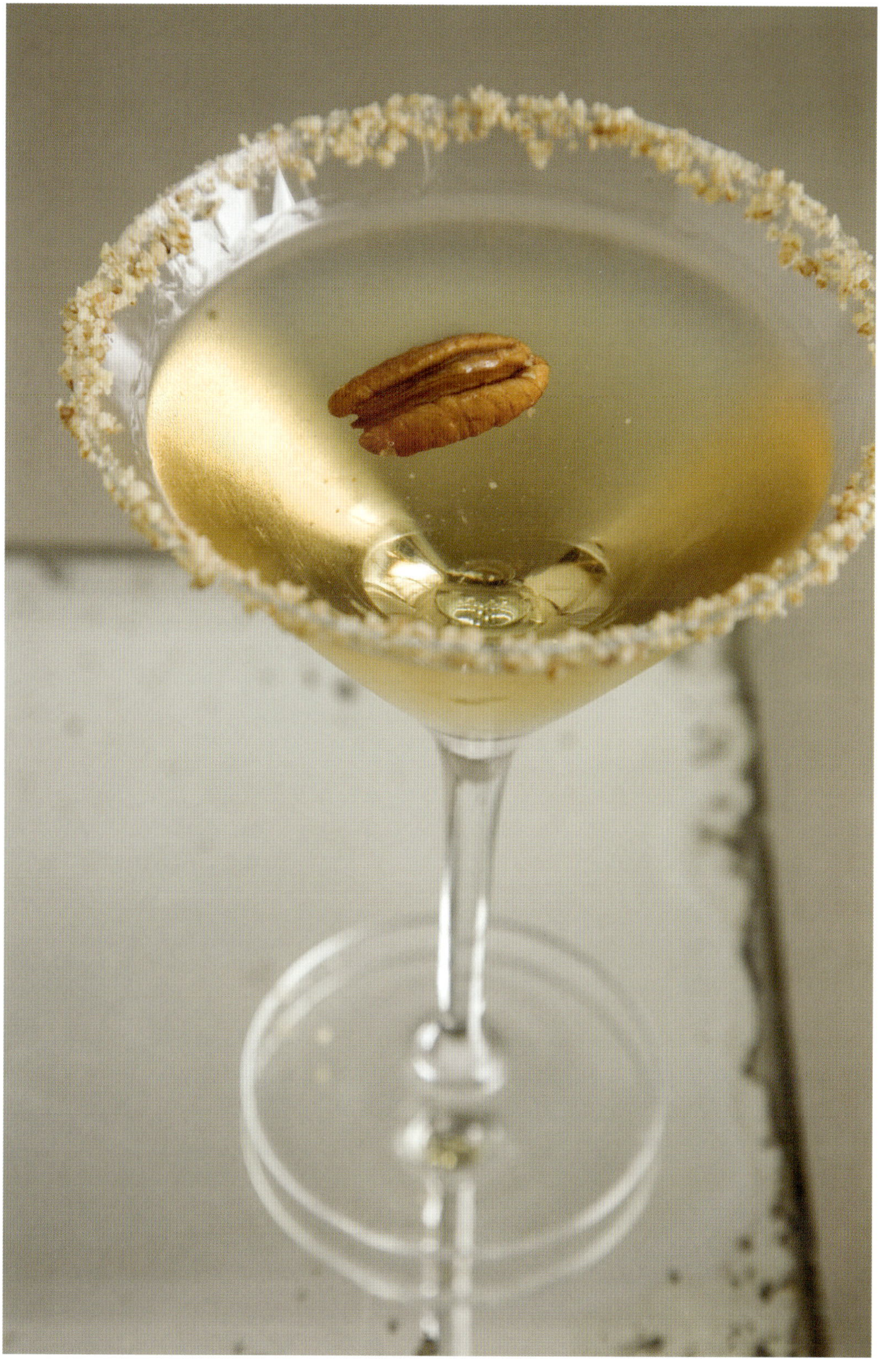

CANE

THE CITY OF
NATCHITOCHES,
LOUISIANA
(EST. 1714)

OAKLAWN PLANTATION

CHEROKEE PLANTATION

...IVER

N

MILES
0 1 2 3 4 5

Index

A
Apple Crisp, 84

B
Baked Pecan Chicken with Lemon Rice Dressing, 44
Banana Bourbon Cake, 86
Banana Split Pie, 90
Basic Roasted Pecans, 22,
Basic Sugared Pecans, 24
Best-Ever Brownies, 100
Broiled Redfish with Pecans and Chili-Roasted Sweet Potatoes, 56
Buttermilk Fudge, 118
Butter Pecan Loaf, 92
Butter Pecan Turtles, 120
Butterscotch Pecan Pie, 108

C
Cheesy Pecan Wafers, 28
Chocolate Orange Pecan Torte, 102
Crab Cakes with Pecan-Butter Sauce and Pecan Bread Dressing, 68
Crabmeat Royale with Pecans and Broccoli with Caramelized Shallots, 72
Cream of Potato and Pecan Soup, 34
Crème Anglaise, 88

D
Deviled Eggs with Pecans, 26

E
Egg Salad with Bacon and Pecans, 36

F
Fig Preserve Cake with Pecan Icing, 98

L
Lemon Chicken with Capers and Pecans and Super-Duper Yams, 52
Les Oreilles de Cochon, 112

M
Macaroon Pie, 104

O
Olivia's Perfect Pecan Pie, 106
Onion Soup with Pecan Crust, 32
Overnight Coffee Cake, 94

P
Pear, Roasted Pecans, and Arugula Salad, 40
Pecan and Chicken Salad, 38
Pecan-Crusted Salmon with Pecan-Breaded Eggplant, 64
Pecan-Ginger Chicken with Pecan Rice Pilaf, 48
Pecan Martini, 124
Pecan Pralines, 116
Pecan Tartlets, 110
Pecan Truffles, 122
Pineapple Cake, 96

R
Rum-Bourbon Balls, 114

S
Shrimp, Vegetable, and Pecan Pasta, 76
Speckled Trout with Pecan Meuniere, Green Beans, and Pecans, 60
Stuffed Pork Chops with Asparagus and Pecan Butter, 78
Sweetened Whipped Cream, 109